2012

Tips on Immigrating to New Zealand

By Travis Haan

ISBN 9781520700823

D1408898

TABLE OF CONTENTS

PHILOSOPHY

INTRODUCTION

The authors of this book are Travis and Amber. We're an American couple who got disillusioned with the American Dream and moved to New Zealand. Shortly after arriving in New Zealand we started a blog called BrokenLuggage.wordpress.com in honor of our luggage that got smashed in transit to New Zealand. Our goal wasn't to give updates on what we did over the weekend but to share all the knowledge we wish we would have known before we left America. This book is a collection of the most useful blog posts from Broken Luggage.

Immigration laws and processes change. So check at http://www.immigration.govt.nz/ for the most up to date information.

IS NEW ZEALAND RIGHT FOR YOU?

If you're considering immigrating to New Zealand then you're probably trying to figure out if New Zealand is better than the place you're at. I can tell you right now that, regardless of where you live, nobody but you can say if New Zealand is better than where you're at. Sure, we can pull up all sorts of empirical statistics about quality of life in New Zealand, but unless you live in a third world or war torn country that really doesn't prove New Zealand is any better than anywhere else because everyone is different and has different priorities. New Zealand might be perfect for your neighbor but not for you.

The real question you need to be asking yourself isn't, "Is New Zealand a good place to live?" You need to be asking yourself, "Is New Zealand right for me?"

Based on my subjective experiences, here are a few factors that indicate immigrating to New Zealand could be right for you.

•You meet the immigration requirements.

•You can cope with being separated from your friends and family.

•You have a high tolerance for change.

•You don't mind a slow pace of life and minor inconveniences such as limited shopping opportunities and slow internet connection.

•You enjoy living with/around people of wildly different cultures and backgrounds.

•You love eating strange foods from different cultures.

•It's important to you that you live in a country with a relatively non-corrupt government.

•You really love the outdoors.

•You really love the ocean.

•You really love to travel.

•It's very important to you that your government not be involved in massive human rights abuses.

•You don't mind taking a pay cut in exchange for lifestyle opportunities.

•You don't mind long winters.

•A safe environment is one of your highest priorities.

•You hate living in a cookie-cutter suburban neighborhood.

These bullet points probably apply to most people like a vague horoscope. I mean, sure, most people like travelling and the outdoors, but do you really, really LOVE to travel and spend time outdoors? If these aren't things you're actively passionate about then you don't really need to move to the other side of the world for them. If you don't really mind living in cookie-cutter houses then you don't really need to turn your life upside down to escape American suburbia. If you're just going to stay inside and watch TV and surf the Internet your entire life, stay where you're at and save your money to buy a bigger TV and computer chair.

I don't say that to sound snide. If that's your passion then focus on it. Moving to a foreign country pushes the reset button on your entire life. You start over from scratch. You have to buy new pillows. You have to learn how to send mail all over again. You have to learn street signs. If you're not seriously dissatisfied with your life or insatiably hungry for a total life challenge then immigrating might be overkill for you.

Here's some signs that New Zealand (or, in some of these cases, immigrating in general) is wrong for you.

•You have very strong ties to your family to the point that your family is your world.

•You're focused like a laser on building your career and making a lot of money.

•It's important to you and your career that you be near the center of the global economy.

•You love the fast life.

•You get mad and frustrated easily.

•You're unfocused at this point in your life and have a hard time committing to anything.

•You can look around you right now and say," Yeah, I've got everything I need right here."

•You thrive on routine.

•You're trying to run away from yourself.

If you're still on the fence, you may consider getting a working holiday visa to New Zealand. You can live here up to 3 years without the hassle/limitations of getting residence or citizenship, but we'll talk about that more later.

YOU DON'T COME TO NEW ZEALAND FOR THE MONEY. YOU COME FOR THE LIFESTYLE

New Zealand has a high cost of living due to the fact that so many products have to be imported, and there isn't competition in the local economy to drive prices down. Plus, New Zealand embraces the island mentality where business isn't (usually) war. So businesses don't stay open late, and the customer isn't always right. This doesn't necessarily mean that life is unaffordable, cumbersome and inconvenient. New Zealand receives thousands of immigrants every year from the South Pacific island, Malaysia, Korea and India where life is certainly harder, but if you compare New Zealand to the United States or Europe, you'll definitely come to miss certain opportunities, luxuries and conveniences.

You're going to work 40 hours per week (sometimes more), but the work culture tends to be more laid back than in America. So you're not as likely to hate going to work as much as in America, but you don't move to New Zealand because you can show up to work in house slippers or have a beer with the boss at lunch. You move here for what goes on after work.

You move to New Zealand to go kayaking at Milford Sound, sunbathing at Whangerei Bay, tasting foods at the Pasifika Festival, skydiving in Taupo, relaxing in Rotorua's hot springs, skiing in Queenstown, surfing in Raglan or fishing anywhere. You come to New Zealand because you can walk down the street without worrying about getting stabbed or shot. You come for the cheap vacation deals to Thailand, Australia, Samoa, Tonga and Indonesia. You come to New Zealand because you don't have to feel guilty for paying taxes to support a predatory industrial war complex. You come here because of the multicultural community and lack of violent racists.

Long story short, you put up with the little worries because you don't have to put up with the major worries that plague the bigger, more volatile, more violent countries. Bottom line, New Zealand is an adventurer/hippie paradise that would be pointless to move to if you're just going to atrophy in your giant suburban home watching 5,000 TV channels shoving your face with big-box processed foods. You come here to get outside and have fun. If you're a die-hard right-wing Republican religious fanatic who hates diversity and loves guns then move to Texas. If you want to live and let live, come to New Zealand and bring your hiking boots with you. Just remember to clean all the dirt off of them first or they'll get quarantined at the airport.

THE PROS OF LIVING IN NEW ZEALAND

•You feel safe. You have to get 2 psych evaluations done before being allowed to buy a gun. You never feel like you need to look over your shoulder here. Point in fact, the other day I saw a gangsta wearing skin-tight Capri pants. No threat there.

•The cops aren't out to get you. They don't even carry guns. In Texas you just take it for granted that there's always going to be a cop around the corner not because they're there to protect you but because they're hunting you, looking for any excuse to bust you for doing nothing in particular so they can meet their ticket quota. Growing up in that environment you just assume that's how life is supposed to be. It's not, and in New Zealand you don't have to live like that.

•The government is relatively un-corrupt. You don't feel the shame and nausea of watching your leaders trample civil rights, reward greed and invade oil rich countries while lying with a straight face about their motives even though everybody knows they're lying. Granted, John Key, the current prime minister, is a bit of a corporate sell out, but at least he doesn't have much power to abuse.

•College costs $5K a year for residents and citizens.

•Healthcare is subsidized. So healthcare is very affordable.

•Prostitution is legal, the age of consent is 16 years old and the drinking age is 18.

•Kiwis aren't (that) obsessed with material goods.

•You'll see billboards and bumper stickers such as: "Airplane fares to Christchurch that won't crucify you!" "94.3 FM: Every other radio station is shit." "Welcome to Raglan! Now leave."

•There are first generation immigrants from all over the world, which makes for a vibrant, multicultural society. This provides a wealth of interesting people to meet and a wide variety of delicious ethnic foods. There are racists in New Zealand, but they're passive-aggressive at worst.

•Kiwis don't hate Americans, just American presidents who are guilty of war crimes.

•Public transportation is decent, and New Zealand doesn't have the stupid zoning laws in America that create suburbs far removed from any shopping, dining, nightlife or work. In New Zealand you can actually walk to places from your house. Not only is this convenient and healthy, but it makes you feel like you're more of a part of your community.

•The culture has a hint of refined British properness to it. This is a breath of fresh air compared to the ignorant, volatile trailer trash rednecks in Texas. However, the Kiwis don't take it to the stifling extreme that say Germans do where you can get a ticket for not washing your windows or you have to wear a suit and tie to get into a nightclub. The Kiwis' refinement is balanced by the laid back Pacific island Aloha mentality. The result is a culture of clean, well-behaved people who don't stress out or take themselves too seriously...most of the time.

•There are a ton of world-class vacation spots within New Zealand that you can visit without spending a lot of money. There's no excuse for not having an adventure in New Zealand.

•Kiwis value traveling. People who travel gain a coherent and intelligent world view. People who have a coherent and intelligent world view make interesting, safe neighbors.

In summary, New Zealand is a little less convenient and a little more expensive than America, but unless you're hopelessly spoiled this really isn't a major hurdle, especially when you consider what you stand to gain by sacrificing those relatively petty amenities. Even without mentioning the stunning beauty, the culture is calmer and saner than America's. My blood pressure has dropped significantly since I got here because I'm not stressed out, afraid and angry at all the trailer trash, gangstas, pushy suburbanites, jocks, valley girls, religious fanatics, sadistic cops and micromanagers who make life miserable in America.

THE CONS OF LIVING IN NEW ZEALAND

•The cost of living is high, particularly the cost of real-estate.

•Alcoholic beverages are taxed by alcohol content. This means that most beers have so little alcohol in them you can drink 15 in one night and just get a stomach ache, and liquor is prohibitively expensive.

•Driving is frustrating. Half the streets don't have any signs telling you their names, and it's completely random how they choose which ones do and don't. When a two lane road becomes one lane there's almost never a sign indicating that this is about to happen. Roads leading to major highways are poorly marked, and on/off ramps are sporadic at best. In the countryside most of the smaller bridges are one lane. Tailgating is socially acceptable.

•The value of the NZ dollar lags behind the U.S. dollar. This is great if you're visiting from Britain. This is bad when you're getting paid minimum wage ($13 NZD per hour).

•You pay for the internet by how many gigabytes of bandwidth you use, and it's about $40 per month for 5 Gigs, which is just enough to check your E-mail and catch up on the news. If you want to watch videos or download any media you'll have to pay $60-$100 per month, and even then you'll still run out of bandwidth by the end of them month. They don't cut your internet off when they happens they just toggle your connection speed down to 56kbs...which means they may as well have just cut it off.

•Bacon, chicken, pickles and popcorn are prohibitively expensive.

•Vegetables get significantly smaller and more expensive in the winter.

•There are no Twizzlers or Reese's Pieces.

•Electronics cost more, and stores offer less variety.

•Shipping anything from overseas is prohibitively expensive.

•Houses usually don't have insulation.

•If you come from an island nation you might be delighted by the wide selection of consumer goods, but coming from America the selection and convenience is slightly stifling.

•Intense UV rays will melt your face off.

•American culture is rapidly invading New Zealand.

HONEST TALK ABOUT SOME OF NEW ZEALAND'S PROBLEMS

1. New Zealand has a bit of a meth problem. They call it "P" here. The reason New Zealand has a meth problem is because it has a poverty problem. Along with meth and poverty comes crime. Granted, these problems radiate out of poor neighborhoods. So if you're wealthy and live in a wealthy neighborhood you'll likely never see these problems. Also, most of the meth use is in the larger cities. So if you live in a quaint little sea side town you're not going to have much trouble. But there are ghettos where crime is a problem. If you don't make a lot of money you'll probably end up living in or near one of those areas, and you'll have to deal with the meth problem.

2. Petty theft is a major problem in New Zealand. Thieves will just walk into your house, grab the first thing of value they see and run out. So it's important to lock your doors...even when you're home. Thieves also target unlocked cars at beaches and parks too. You see "Lock it or Lose it" signs at every tourist destination.

3. Kiwis like to fight, and they're pretty big people. So fights can get serious quick. Plus, since this is such a social country and everyone goes out with their mates to get on the piss, there's a good chance that if you spend enough time out on the town you're going to cross paths with a group of drunken trouble makers eventually who don't mind ganging up on an opponent. There's a biker gang in New Zealand called "The Mongrel Mob" that takes shit from no one. There are some high school gangs too, but they're more likely to cuss at you from across the street. But if you cuss back you might end up with a dozen 16 year olds kicking you in the back. Large groups of teenagers have even ganged up on police officers (who don't usually carry firearms).

4. Racism in New Zealand is a peculiar thing. It seems like everyone is a little bit racist. It's certainly only a matter of time before you hear racist talk and people complaining about immigrants. However, almost nobody acts on their racism. However, a lot of employers require job applicants to have 1-3 years New Zealand work experience. This is a thinly veiled excuse to weed-out immigrants from the job pool.

5. New Zealand is a relatively small nation at the bottom of the world. The size of the economy reflects this. You don't have a lot of choices in the products you buy, and the prices for those products are high. That's life. Living in New Zealand is a lot like living in Italy. You have to adapt to a slower pace of life with less options. If you can't live without a Starbucks in your 24 hour Wal-Mart Super Center you won't be able to make it in New Zealand.

THE REALITY OF KIWI AUSTERITY

As a general rule I'll stand by my statement that if you move to New Zealand you'll live in a relatively stable, civilized country. You can let your guard down here and sleep soundly at night. If you live in Uganda or Compton I can pretty much guarantee that New Zealand would feel like Utopia to you, and you probably wouldn't even notice the first world problems all the white people around you are always angry about. However, if you currently live in a giant house in a mega-burb outside an American mega city and have central heating and air conditioning, a huge back yard and every super store imaginable within a 15 minute drive (that are all open 24 hours a day) then you're going to experience a significant loss in your quality of life as measured by material standards if you move to New Zealand.

To enjoy the safety, beauty and culture of New Zealand you're probably going to have to accept a slightly lower quality of life by material standards. Unless you're working in upper management or a highly technical, understaffed career field then there's a realistic possibility you're going to have to wear a sweater or two around the house during the winter.

That might not sound like a big deal until you wake up at 6:30 in the morning and it's dead cold in your room and your electric blanket turned itself off hours ago. So you don't want to move because you don't want to lose any of the heat you have trapped under your blanket. But you have to go to work. So after working up the courage, you dash from your bed to the shower skipping on your tip-toes because the wood floor is freezing. Then you wedge yourself into a cold, ceramic shower and turn on the water and wait for it to heat up while you squirm like an alien. Then you don't want to get out of the shower because it's cold out there and you're all wet and you know you're just going to snap-freeze as soon as you get out of the shower and you know you're not going to dry yourself completely because you'll be in too much of a hurry to get your warm clothes on. Plus, since the humidity never drops below London fog your towels are permanently damp and asthma-inducing, sinus-infecting mold grows on all the windowsills. So you end up going to work feeling a swamp beast.

Then on your way to work in the morning, you stop to get gas and pay $9 a gallon to fill up your micro car. You take solace from these problems though by reminding yourself that you have really cheap healthcare, which is important because you're not getting enough vitamins since bell peppers and squash cost $4 a piece in the winter, and 3 boneless, skinless chicken breasts cost $14 when they're on sale. And since the stores don't stock much variety of anything you're basically eating the same ten meals over and over again unless you can find some hole in the wall ethnic market to shop in.

At least it's easy to blend in because everyone you see at any gas station is wearing the same clothes as you that you all bought at the same three department stores, and those stores are just selling all the old leftover stock American department stores had left over from the 80s.

If any of this bothers you, you won't be able to smoke and/or drink your brain into a comatose state where you don't realize you're broke all the time because cigarettes cost $16 per pack and alcohol costs $16 a six pack.

When you put it all together it's kind of a big deal. It just never really hit me because I'm used to being completely broke all the time. I hate to say it, but if you're poor, white trash you'll likely find New Zealand an easy place to live. Case in point, in New Zealand it's normal to walk around the city and into stores barefoot. I suspect this is also why there are so many hippies in New Zealand. They're used to scraping by below the poverty level, and they want to spend their weekends and vacations going on grand adventures to green places. So they stay. The kind of Kiwis who detest hippies tend to move to Australia where they can make more money and enjoy more sun.

I hate to put a specific number on this. I don't know how New Zealand defines the poverty line, but I see lots of people making $60,000 per year eating wilted vegetables and living in cold, rickety houses where everyone gathers around the space heater at night. If you make $30,000 per year you'll definitely be living like that.

I can't guarantee that if you move to New Zealand you'll ever experience any of this. All I'm saying is that I've looked around, and I've seen a lot of it. If you want to learn more about Kiwi austerity, see what real Kiwis have to say about this article.

IS NEW ZEALAND A GOOD PLACE TO RAISE CHILDREN?

Is New Zealand a good place to raise Children? The short answer is, yes.

New Zealand is a very safe place to raise children. Your child has a higher chance of drowning or dying in a car accident than they do of being shot or kidnapped. Gangs aren't very big in New Zealand, and most of the gangs New Zealand does have are made up of posers who just listened to too much rap music. The exception is the Mongrel Mob, but as a foreigner, your kid probably wouldn't be welcome in the Mongrel Mob anyway.

The school system is pretty good. Kids get a broad education with lots of opportunities for vocational training, travel, cultural activities, sports and academic competitions in addition to standard academic classes. Unfortunately, New Zealand schools are starting to follow America's example of valuing standardized testing over true education. All I can say is that I hope that failed experiment gets shut down sooner rather than later. In the meantime...you've been warned, that plague has already spread to New Zealand, but it's not as crippling as it is in America...yet.

Most (if not all) schools in New Zealand require students to wear uniforms that look like cheap bell hop or nurses uniforms from a low budget Hollywood movie, and the girls wear (what I call) pedo skirts. They do this because of the lingering British influence in New Zealand culture/institutions. Discipline in schools is pretty good, but there are always underfunded, bad schools with incompetent administrators who fear parents more than they respect the importance of discipline. You can check the Ministry of Education's decile rankings to see if a school is good enough for your kids.

Hard drugs exist in New Zealand, but they're hard to get and very expensive. So New Zealand doesn't have as vibrant of a drug culture as larger, mainland countries. Marijuana is pretty easy to get, and it's very potent. You've been warned. Cigarettes are prohibitively expensive ($16 per pack). So your kids probably won't be able to afford them even if they wanted them. Alcohol is legal to buy at 18. So there's quite of a bit of high school drinking, but it's no worse than in America. You're just going to have to make sure you have plenty of productive talks with your children about the dangers of alcohol. The age of sexual consent in New Zealand is 16 years old, but the culture still frowns upon adults sleeping with teens.

The best part about being a child in New Zealand is getting to enjoy all the camping, hiking, oceans, rivers, hot springs and other tourist attractions New Zealand has to offer. New Zealand is a giant backyard. Adults travel from all over the world to come play in New Zealand. Kids who get to grow up here are lucky as hell to get to enjoy so many fun activities in such a small place.

I think New Zealand might actually be wonderful to a fault. I've met a surprisingly large number of Kiwis with serious anger issues who get unreasonably mad at the slightest first world problem. At first I thought there might be something in the water that made Kiwis angry. Then I thought there might have been too much inbreeding that affected Kiwis' brains. Now I'm convinced it's just that a lot of Kiwis grow up with such little hardship in their lives that they have no frame of reference to understand that little problems aren't worth getting screaming mad over. So if you raise children in New Zealand, make sure to take them on a vacation to someplace really terrible so they can learn some perspective.

One legitimate problem New Zealand does pose for children is that it's so isolated. This motivates some Kiwi-raised kids to want to spread their wings and see the world when they're old enough. It's even semi-expected of children to go on an OE (overseas experience) after high school. Certainly, growing up in New Zealand will expose you to people from every nationality around the world on a nearly daily basis. This is fantastic for cultivating an open-minded world perspective that just isn't possible in say, West Texas. However, the isolation gets to some kids. Growing up in an isolated culture makes them identify as small-town backwoods hicks who are disconnected from the world at large. This can make them lethargic, especially since life in New Zealand is so great. You see this in kids in Hawaii. There's a tendency to just accept where you are and never set your sights higher.

In fact, there's a cultural phenomenon in New Zealand called "Tall Poppy Syndrome." In America you're expected to be the next celebrity superstar. In New Zealand overachievers are often seen as show-offs who need to be taken down a notch. Kids who grow up enforcing the Tall Poppy Syndrome enter the workforce and continue to act like underachievers.

As a result, corporate culture in New Zealand is a general disaster. It's fun to work here if you're looking for a laid back lifestyle, but if you came to succeed you're going to run into brick walls constantly. Obviously, this isn't universal in New Zealand, but it's a big enough phenomenon that it would be negligent of me not to warn you about. So if you do bring children to New Zealand you need to talk to them about motivation.

I don't want to make New Zealand sound like it has an unchecked podunk, backwoods culture. It has a brilliantly vibrant, diverse culture. It's a colorful place with colorful people. It's a melting pot where your children will be exposed to an entire world of ideas, but you have to get your kid out of the house and into the flow of life to experience it all.

One last great thing about raising kids in New Zealand that I want to mention is that once they get their citizenship they can still (usually) keep their birth country's citizenship, and I believe if they're born in New Zealand they'll get to be dual citizens in New Zealand and their parent's birth country. This opens up global job opportunities that aren't easily available to say, someone who only has American citizenship. With a New Zealand citizenship you can sail right over to Australia and make good money in their growing economy. You're also a member of the British Commonwealth, which makes it slightly easier for your children to work in those countries after they graduate.

New Zealand has its share of problems. It has produced its share of idiots. If you follow New Zealand politics you'll see that. But I blame those idiots' parents more than I blame New Zealand. In my personal opinion, I believe New Zealand is a great place to raise kids. It's safe, fun and provides ample opportunities to set up children for success in life.

IS THE GRASS REALLY GREENER?

The following events have happened in the United States since I left there and moved to New Zealand:

The Sikh Temple Shooting

The Colorado Batman shooting

Chick-Fil-A inequality appreciation day

Herman Cain was almost president.

Rick Perry was almost president.

Obamacare made me facepalm

Obama turned out to be George Bush 2.0

Jersey Shore happened

America was selling weapons to Mexican drug cartels, and the president stepped in censored it from the public.

The Westboro Baptist church is still doing its thing.

It surprised nobody when it was made public that mulched gristle sprayed with ammonia was commonly added to the meat products everyone consumes.

It turned out soda causes cancer. It also turned out that's no big deal.

Occupy Wall Street movement protested corruption in government and was brutally suppressed by the police.

On the upside, America landed another Rover on Mars. Granted, we could have people living on Mars by now if NASA had received all the money the United States military has spent fighting in the Middle East.

Sure, Osama Bin Laden's death was a cause to celebrate, or breathe a sigh of relief at least, but if the best thing that happened to you all year involved dumping bodies in the ocean then fuck your life.

You want to know what's going on in New Zealand?

There was a dead possum pageant that upset a few folks

The All Blacks won the 2011 Rugby World Cup

And that's about it.

I'm not trying to prove in a list of articles that New Zealand is better than the United States. All I'm saying is, every once and a while, I see something that makes me stop and say, "Gee. I'm glad I'm not there anymore." From my own personal, subjective perspective the grass in America still looks pretty wilted. New Zealand's grass is pretty green.

HOW DID YOU DO IT?

Since we started blogging about moving to New Zealand a lot of people have written to us and asked us, "How did you do it?" I totally understand where this question is coming from. When you first start thinking about moving to a new country it seems like an impossible feat... like you have to activate a Stargate to move to escape your birth country. Granted, it's not easy; there are a lot of hoops you have to jump through, but at the end of the day all it really amounts to is going to the New Zealand immigration website and filling out a bunch of forms and getting a medical physical.

But really, that's it. You fill out the bureaucratic paperwork, you wait a long time to get it approved, you pay a bunch of money in fees, and eventually you get to move to another country. You don't have to take a ring to Mordor. You just have to fill out a bunch of paperwork. That's all you have to do. I wish someone would have slapped us in the face when we started our immigration process and said, "Don't stress out about it so much! Just fill out the paperwork and send it! You fill out tax paperwork every year. Fill out a few more papers and get going!" Hell, you can go through the whole process (expect the medical examination) drunk.

Plus, there's no commitment necessary. It's not like joining the military. If you think you might want to immigrate to New Zealand then go to the New Zealand Immigration website, make an account and start the process. If at some point you find out you're not eligible then the worst thing that will happen is you get told "no." You might spend a little money in the process, but you probably would have spent that money on junk you didn't need anyway.

If you do get approved, but at the last minute you decide that you don't want to take the leap of moving, then don't move! You don't renounce your citizenship when you apply for residency. You don't even renounce your citizenship after you've been approved and you physically move. Even after you get your citizenship you'll be a dual citizen unless you go out of your way to renounce your citizenship from your birth country.

Amber and I had never visited New Zealand before we moved here, and we didn't know anyone living here. A lot of people thought we were crazy for taking such an insane risk, but the only thing we were really risking was the money we spent. We went into the affair understanding that if we didn't like New Zealand then we could always just move back to America. You could say the money we spent in the process could have been wasted, but we would say the money was well spent on an adventure that taught us a lot about ourselves and the world we live in. Fortunately for us, we're happy in New Zealand and have never regretted moving, but that's just icing on the cake. If it had turned out that we hated New Zealand (which it very well could have) we still could have moved back to our birth country not feeling like idiots. So can you.

Yes, there were risks in moving to a foreign country, but there are risks in doing anything. There was a Twilight Zone episode where a woman refuses to leave her house for fear of anything bad happening to her. Finally, a man collapses outside her house, and she ventures outside to help him. It turns out he's a wonderful person, and she enjoys the experience it brings her to interact with the outside world. In Twilight Zone fashion though, the man turns out to be the Grim Reaper, and he makes her realize she's wasted her life hiding from life for fear of the consequences. Amber and I did the cost-benefit-analysis of hiding in cold comfort in America or sticking our necks out and moving to New Zealand. We took the risk, and it paid off for us. But even if it hadn't paid off in a long-term place of residence, it still would have paid off in the experience. And all it took to get here was filling out a bunch of paperwork and paying a bunch of fees.

The point is, don't make the process harder than it is. All you're doing it filling out a bunch of paperwork, and all you're doing is moving from one place on this rock to another. You're not moving to another universe. There are cars and streets and houses over here just like there is where you were born. If you do fill out the application or even make the move your decision will still be less final, and less costly, than deciding to marry someone. If you have the courage to marry then you have more than enough courage to move to another spot on the earth.

STEPS TO APPLY FOR PERMANENT RESIDENCY

This isn't the only path to residency, but I think it's the path most people will take. These instructions assume you're using the "skilled migrant work-to-residence path" and you don't already have a job lined up in New Zealand prior to entering the country.

Step One – Have your qualifications (i.e. Degrees and certifications) assessed by the NZQA (New Zealand Qualification Authority).

Step Two – Decide what visa you want to apply for.

Step Three – Submit your EOI (Expression of Intent). This is you asking NZ if you can apply to immigrate to NZ.

Step Four – After your EOI has been selected you will be sent the real application form. This is where you tell the NZ Immigration board your life story. And you'll need to get a police certificate and medical physical. Turn all of this in as soon as possible. This will sit for 90 days before being looked at. Only then will you be notified of a problem/question with your application.

Step Five- Your phone interview.

Step Six – Acceptance/Rejection

Step Seven- Get a working holiday visa.

Step Eight- Move to New Zealand

Step Nine- Go to the post office and get an I.R.D. card (Internal Revenue Department) so you can legally work.

Step Ten – Get a job.

Step Eleven- Get your permanent worker's visa.

Step Twelve- Live in New Zealand for two years.

Step Thirteen – Apply for permanent residency.

Step Fourteen- Live in New Zealand for two more years and then apply for citizenship.

WHAT IF YOU DON'T QUALIFY FOR PERMANENT RESIDENCY?

Disclaimer (again): We're not professional immigration consultants. So don't base your life on our advice. Research the New Zealand Immigration site. Use your own judgment, and don't break the law.

If you're not in perfect health, and you don't have a bachelor's degree then you probably don't qualify to immigrate to New Zealand through the skilled migrant's work-to-residence program. In that case here are some tips to get into New Zealand legally.

1. Get married to someone (from your home country) who is qualified. Point in fact, I (Travis) didn't qualify to move to New Zealand because I'm a year short of a university degree. However, Amber has a degree in teaching. So she's qualified. When married couples file for immigration you'll list one person as the primary applicant, and that's the person who will be judged. Whatever else the secondary applicant brings to the table is just icing on the cake, and if they don't bring anything to the table you're not penalized for it. Either way, be warned that you have to be married for two years prior to submitting your application. New Zealand recognizes common law marriages as well. Just make sure you have 2 years' worth of shared bills, bank accounts, E-mails, vacation photos and anything else that proves you're connected at the hip.

2. Get a degree. Every accredited university is equal in the eyes of the immigration board. You won't get any extra points for going to Harvard than you will for going to Joe Bob's University. This means you can take advantage of diploma mills like The University of Phoenix, which offer relatively easy online classes and gives you credit for life experiences. Using accredited

diploma mills like this will allow you to punch out a degree relatively quickly. And make sure to check out the Essential Skills in Demand list. Getting a degree in one of these fields will give you extra points towards your application. Be aware that this list is updated regularly.

3. Fall in love with a local. As hard as it is to immigrate anywhere you'd think the entire world would collapse if one more person moved to a new country, but for all the red tape involved in keeping you in your birth country, there's a gigantic back door that will let you waltz right into to just about any country. If you fall in love with a person from a foreign country you can bypass most of the legal requirements.

Now, marrying solely for the purpose of obtaining citizenship is illegal. So when you get a holiday visa or a working holiday visa and visit your prospective country and go to the first bar you see and ask the first 30 people you see if they'll fall in love with you, make sure your love is real. As long as you really care about the person you just met, your mutually beneficial partnership will be completely legal. Be warned though, you have to go through a pretty lengthy process of proving to the immigration board that your love is real. This involves years' worth of references, photos, financial ties and a bunch of other stuff I don't know about. Again, make sure your love is real. Don't break the law.

4. The Hail Mary. The whole purpose of making the immigration process so difficult is to keep freeloaders with no viable job skills out of any given country. If you can prove you have job skills they'll let you in, but you'll still need a job offer before your residency visa gets its final approval. This means you have to apply for your residency visa, pass the preliminary approvals

and then get a job offer. However, nobody is going to give you a job offer while you live in your birth country unless you have amazing and/or rare credentials since New Zealand businesses have ten people standing right outside their door who can start work tomorrow. It doesn't make any sense for them to go out of their way to sponsor a stranger from a foreign country who can't start work until they sell everything they own and move half way around the world.

As a result, you're going to have to move to New Zealand (or wherever) on a working holiday visa (while your residency visa is still half-approved), apply for jobs and hopefully get one before your working holiday visa runs out. If/when you get that job you can then get your permanent work permit approved. Two years later you can apply to get your permanent residency approved.

Now here's the interesting part. You can move to New Zealand on a working holiday visa, get a job and then apply for your permanent work permit/permanent residency. Since you're already in the country and you already have a job you've already proven to the immigration board that they're not letting a freeloader into the country even if you don't have the most impressive credentials. This will make the immigration paperwork a little easier and a little quicker. However, this is a very dangerous tightrope to walk. You can still fail your residency application if you have bad health or if they don't deem your work skills sufficient. For example, getting a job at McDonald's won't impress the immigration board. If your job falls under the Essential Skills in Demand list then you'll have the best chance of getting your residency visa approved.

There are probably other factors I'm not aware of that could affect your application, but if you're really desperate and you're willing to take a risk, this path could potentially work. If nothing else, you could genuinely fall in love with one of your coworkers while you're in country and legally use the marriage loophole to get your citizenship.

5. Get Rich Quick. Laws and restrictions are for poor people. If you can get $3 million in your bank account the immigration board will roll out the red carpet for you.

6. Get Professional Help. The process of immigrating to New Zealand is stressful enough that a small industry has bloomed to help people through the immigration process….for a fee of course. If you need professional help, then help is just a Google search away.

What if none of these legal loopholes apply to you? Too bad. You don't get to leave your home country. All the governments of the world have colluded to set the bar to immigration so high that they've effectively made the poor and loveless prisoners in their birth country, and they've done it in a way that every country can claim plausible deniability. That's the way of the world, and statistically speaking you're probably one of the billions of humans beings whose fate and tax dollars are imprisoned within your national borders.

THE WORKING HOLIDAY VISA

You can live in a foreign country for 1-3 years pretty easily. All you have to do is get a working holiday visa. It's staying in a country permanently that takes a ton of paperwork and thousands of dollars in fees.

I've met hundreds of people from all over the world who have taken 6 months to 3 years out of their old lives to live and work in a foreign country, and frankly, some of them were pretty damned dumb. It's really not that difficult. If you can move from one city to another city in your home country you'd be surprised how capable you are of moving to a city in another country. The general public just doesn't seem to grasp how realistic an option working temporarily in another country is.

I'll explain the steps to living and working temporarily in New Zealand, but this advice is pretty universal.

Step 0: Get a passport. If you can't figure out how to get a passport then don't worry about moving to a foreign country. Despite what I said two paragraphs ago, you're too dumb to survive in a foreign country.

Step 1: Fill out and submit the paperwork to get a working holiday visa. A working holiday visa to New Zealand was $120 NZ last time I checked. You can afford that. You'll also need to get a medical physical done. Do you know how to schedule a physical? You call your doctor, set an appointment, take 30 minutes out of your day to have some blood drawn, and then you wait for your results. You might pay around $200 for your physical for a working holiday visa. You might pay $500 for your physical for a permanent residency visa.

Step 2: Buy a plane ticket. Once you get your working holiday visa all that's left to do is buy a plane ticket. If you keep your schedule open, watch the prices of flights and don't leave at the busiest travel time of the year you'd be surprised how cheap you can get around the world. $900 will get you almost anywhere if you can wait. Otherwise, $1,500 will get you anywhere if you book it just a little early.

3. Go to the airport. Then go sit on a plane. Eat a hot meal, watch a bad children's movie and then get off the plane. Walk out of the new airport you find yourself in. Walk to the street curb and hail a taxi.

4. Get a place to stay. Tell the taxi driver to take you to the 3rd cheapest hostel in town. Trust me, no matter what city you go to you don't want to stay at the two worst hostels in town. Go cheap, but don't stay at a death trap.

In New Zealand, a very popular alternative to staying in a hostel is to buy a camper van or station wagon that is fully furnished to live out of for backpacking/camping purposes. There's always a few for sale on www.trademe.co.nz. Chances are your hostel will have fliers posted from travelers trying to sell the camper they bought for their trip that is now over. I've met one or two people who sold their travel van for a profit at the end of their vacation. Note: this may not be safe in every country....but it is in New Zealand.

5. Get a job. If you stay at a hostel you might find fliers for people looking for backpackers to do seasonal work. Otherwise, you'll probably meet someone who knows where to find it. If you were smart you would have found out where all the work is before you arrived. If not you can spend your days walking down the street with a stack full of resumes giving them to every shop on every street. Or you can pay $2 per hour to surf

the internet at an internet cafe doing Google searches for "Seasonal Work" "Fruit Pickers" and "Kitchen staff."

And that's it. That's how millions of people travel the world and live in foreign countries. You just submit an application for a visa, buy a plane ticket, go there, get a place to stay and then find a job. It doesn't take a superhuman feat to accomplish. Regular people are quite capable of this. Once you've got the hang of it, you can just hop from country to country for years without stopping. Note: You probably won't be able to save any money for retirement during that time though. So think carefully about how long you do this for.

The hard part about spending 1-3 years in a foreign country is paying for it. But let's break down the cost and see how much it really is:

$120 for the visa.

$200 for the medical physical

$300 for backpack and travel gear

$1000 for a plane ticket

$400 per month rent

$100 per week for food

$300 for things you're going to ignorantly pay too much for before you learn the ropes in the new city you're in

$100 per week for having fun

So basically it's going to cost about $2500 to get into the country and get a roof over your head. Once you've accomplished that you just need about $1000 for every month you expect to be unemployed. However, that can be reduced by $400 per month if you live in a camper van. However, you'll have to bring an extra $1500-$4000 to buy the van.

Assuming you don't buy a camper van it'd be ideal to allow yourself 3 months to find a job. It shouldn't take that long unless you procrastinate, but it's better to be safe than sorry, and this will allow you to be a little pickier about what job you take. So plan to bring $3,000 for living expenses.

That brings the total cost of moving to a foreign country to $5,500 (assuming you can find a job in 3 months). Throw in traveler's insurance, emergency money and the possibility that you might have to prove you have at least $5000 in your bank account before you're granted a working holiday visa and we'll just call the grand total $7500. Of course, the more you bring the more options and less stress you'll have. Actually, this whole price list is moot because in order to qualify for a working holiday visa you have to prove you have $10,000 available in your bank account. But the immigration board set that requirement because it's a few thousand dollars more than a frugal traveler realistically needs.

So here's what it all comes down to. I can't say if you should move to another country for 1-3 years or not, but if it's a dream of yours then the only thing standing between it and you is $10,000 and a round trip plane ticket. How much is that really? You can save that much. If you don't have that kind of money, ask yourself what luxuries you could sacrifice to get it. You're probably pissing most of your money away on frivolous things anyway. Would it be worth sacrificing some of those unnecessary indulgences for 6 months to 1 year to have the experience of a lifetime?

All I'm saying is that it has been done, and you can probably do it too if you tried.

SEASONAL FRUIT WORK ON A WORKING HOLIDAY VISA

Note: Everything said here is true about Australia also.

New Zealand has an interesting option available to international travelers under the age of 30 to help them live, work and play in the country for a year or longer. I'm talking about the temporary work visa, but temporary work visas aren't unique to New Zealand. You can get a temporary work visa to most countries. The problem is finding a job once you get there. Job hunting in a country you don't know anything about is an intimidating task especially if you're doing it while going through the throws of culture shock. If you're dedicated and resourceful you can work in pretty much any country, but most people don't have the world traveling experience and grit to navigate all the obstacles to working in a foreign country.

New Zealand offers an easy way to sidestep most of the hassle of finding temporary work: by doing seasonal farm work. You don't need experience or a resume to do most seasonal farm work. You don't need an interview, and you don't have to comb through the classifieds section of the Sunday paper to find job vacancies. There are job boards you can access on the internet that will help you find work, and some of them may require resumes, but these jobs boards are pretty easy to use:

http://www.bbh.co.nz/travellers/billboards.asp?b=7

http://www.backpackerboard.co.nz/

http://www.picknz.co.nz

The absolute easiest way to find seasonal work in New Zealand though is by staying at a working backpacker hostel, and there are a lot of good reasons to stay at these places anyway. Firstly, they're cheap, costing between $15-$40 per night or $100-$160 per week, and there are often discounts for paying by the month or having a BBH club card. Since most of the other guests are travelers you'll get to meet people from all over the world, and since you'll be staying there working for weeks or months you'll have plenty of time to make close friends you may keep for the rest of your life. It's not uncommon for backpackers to make new friends and then end up traveling all over the country with them. Some even pair up to travel to other countries. It's also worth mentioning that a lot of them have sex, and some of them get married.

None of that would be possible if the hostels didn't find their guests jobs. The way they find work for their guests is by building working relationships with the contractors and farmers in their local area. So when farms need workers they call the hostel to recruit workers or the hostel will go through their Rolodex and call every farmer within 50 miles until they find work for their guests. But the guests don't care how they get a job. All they have to do is check in, let the manager know they're looking for work and wait for a job to fall in their lap. Before you can start work though you'll need a copy of your passport, valid temporary work visa, I.R.D. number and a New Zealand bank account. If you're missing any of those documents the hostel manager should be able to help you get them.

Below is a list of working backpacker hostels in New Zealand. If anyone knows of any that are missing from this list feel free to leave a comment.

Hawkes Bay Region

The Rotten Apple: www.rottenapple.co.nz

Marlborough Region

Duncannon: www.duncannon.co.nz

Happy Apple: www.happyapplebackpackers.co.nz

Lemon Tree: www.backpackersblenheim.co.nz

Leeways: www.leeways.byethost22.com

Northland Region

Hone Heke Lodge: www.honeheke.co.nz

Kiwi Bunk House: www.kiwibunkhouse.co.nz

Cherry Camp: http://www.cherrycamp.co.nz/

Central Lodge: www.centrallodgenz.com

Tauranga Region

Harbourside City Backpackers: www.backpacktauranga.co.nz

Bell Lodge: www.bell-lodge.co.nz

Hairy Berry Backpacker: www.hairyberrynz.com

Just the Ducks Nuts: www.justtheducksnuts.co.nz

Depending on the region, these hostels can help you find work picking apples, grapes, peaches, plums, pears, cherries, kiwi fruit and blueberries. The work is hard. It will make your body hurt, but it will make you grow as a person, and it'll teach you the value of a hard day's work. If you're not physically fit you can try to find work in a packhouse where you just stand at a conveyor belt and sort/pack all the fruit your mates picked in the orchards. Sometimes you can also find work in wine factories doing things like putting labels on bottles.

Some of these jobs pay minimum wage, and some of them pay "by contract," which means you get paid by how many bins you fill with fruit or by how many plants you prune. Farmers will tell you that you can make up to $200 per day on contract, but that assumes you're in peak physical condition and there's plenty of fruit in the orchards/vineyards. It does happen, but as a general rule, $120 per day is a more realistic average. If you make less than minimum wage you're still supposed to get paid minimum wage, but your farmer probably won't give minimum wage to a contract worker unless you report them to the labor department.

If you find yourself working for a dishonest farmer you can always just quit and go work somewhere else. Since seasonal employers don't ask for resumes they won't care why you left your last job. They'll just be glad you have fruit picking experience. Once you've worked and played in one region of New Zealand for a few months you can move to another region, do more work and save your money until you're ready to spend a few months traveling around New Zealand with the backpackers you've met along the way.

Doing seasonal work in New Zealand is a wild experience, but be aware that you can only get one temporary work visa to New Zealand (though you can extend your work visa a few months). If you want to get your permanent residency in New Zealand you'll have to secure a job. You can't secure a job without a work visa. If you've already used your temporary work visa doing seasonal work you won't be able to use it to find a permanent job when you go for your permanent residency. So be aware of that.

12 TIPS FOR MOVING TO A FOREIGN COUNTRY

1. Do your research. The first few weeks of your trip are going to be the hardest. You're going to experience culture shock. You're going to feel lost. You're going to feel alone and vulnerable. Everything is going to be unknown to you, and it's going to be overwhelming. This is inevitable, but it can be minimized by doing your research prior to moving. What should you research? Everything. Read every single book you can find about the place you're going. Read travel sites, expat sites, newspapers from the place you're going to. Anything you can learn to familiarize yourself with the place you're going to will help make it easier to transition into. Ideally, you should visit the place you're going before moving there. If you can't do that then take a virtual tour on Google Street Maps.

2. Get a working holiday Visa. Don't move to a new country on a holiday visa and expect to be able to find work. Even if you've applied for a residence visa you still need a job before your residency will be approved, and you can't work on a holiday visa. On the other hand, if you get a working holiday visa then you can work, and if you're a good enough worker your employer might extend your working holiday visa another year or flat out sponsor you for residency. None of that can happen on a regular holiday visa.

3. Get everything squared away at home before leaving. Any unfinished business at home (especially involving bills) will be ten times harder to deal with from a foreign country, and with all the stress and the unknowns you're going to be dealing with already, you don't need that extra monumental headache in your life. Don't rush off to your grand adventure. Take the extra

time to square away any paperwork, bills, contracts or other obligations you may have at home before leaving.

4. Lower your expectations. Have you ever been to see a movie that you thought was sure to be awesome only to find out it was mediocre and you hated it? Have you ever been to a movie you were sure was going to suck only to find out it really wasn't that bad and you left feeling fairly impressed even though the movie wasn't really that great? Moving to another country is the same way. If you're moving to another country you obviously believe it's a place worth moving to and is for some reason preferable to the place you're at. However, I guarantee it's not going to be perfect. There are going to be downsides to it. If you go into your journey expecting to find the land of milk and honey you're going to be sorely disappointed. If you go into it fully prepared to experience disappointment you're going to be far less disappointed, and in the end, you're going to have a more positive experience.

5. Bring at least $20,000. (This figure is in US dollars. Convert accordingly.) The number one cause of stress and ultimately failure when moving to a foreign country is money problems. The less money you bring the harder your life is going to be, the less secure you're going to feel, the fewer leisure options you'll have and the less time you'll have to find a job. Between exchange rate fees, government fees, rental deposits, utility bills, food, transportation, leisure activities and buying toiletries, basic necessities you couldn't fit in your suitcase and especially unforeseen expenses, you should really bring at least $20,000 with you or else you're going to be extremely stressed during what will probably already be the most stressful experience you've ever had. You might still make it, but the more money

you bring the better off you'll be in every way. We made our move on $15,000, and barely scraped by.

6. Find temporary lodging at your new location and be prepared to move. Make accommodation reservations before you leave your home country so you'll have a place to check into when your plane lands. However, don't book it for more than a month. It might turn out to be a horrible environment. It might also turn out to be far away from where you want/need to be. So give yourself some leeway to move around a bit as you get your bearings. Also, don't stop moving around until you've found someplace comfortable. I hate to keep harping on how stressful moving to another country is, but stress is inevitable. The only question is how stressful you're going to make your life. Living in a place far away from where you want/need to be, living with roommates you don't like in a cramped apartment that irritates your allergies where you have no furniture is going to seriously hurt your chances of happiness and ultimately success. If the first place you unpack your bags at isn't working for you, get out of there and find a place that does work for you.

7. Get the Internet. Bring a laptop with you. Other than your passport, nothing else is more important than that, and anything else you had to leave out of your luggage can be bought cheaply on the local market. If you can, try to stay at some place that provides free internet connection. If the place you're at doesn't have the internet, get it. You're going to need the internet to stay in contact with your family and friends, look up bus schedules, buy a car, find a job, meet people, learn about the local area and a hundred other vital things you wouldn't predict. You're going to be lost without the internet. So just go ahead and put that at the top of your list of things to do when you arrive in country. Granted, you can still use

Internet cafes, but those are a pain in the ass. Avoiding Internet cafes will lower your stress level. And make sure to have Skype on your computer. Being able to make free video calls home to your loved ones will be priceless. Having a smartphone with GPS will also make your life 10 times easier.

8. Network. Once you get on the Internet find some meet-up groups in your local area. The best case scenario is to meet other expats. Nobody is going to be more helpful than other people who have already walked in your shoes or are walking in them right now. I know you probably can't wait to meet the locals, but your fellow countrymen are going to be more eager to help, and they'll lessen the culture shock. Having said that, you should definitely also join meet-up groups with the locals. It'll be fun. It'll help you transition into the new culture and you'll meet people who can offer you inside information.

9. Similar to #8, ask the locals. Inevitably you're going to have a lot of questions that need answers when you get to your new country. How do I find a job? How do I use the bus? How do I buy a car? How do I apply for any of the dozens of forms and applications I need to apply for? You can find all these answers after hours of research on the Internet or you can walk down to the gas station and ask a local. Typically they'll be more than happy to point you in the right direction. If you have a question, save yourself some time and just ask a local.

10. Get out of the house. No matter how prepared you are to move to a new country there will always be unknowns. The unknown will be the scariest part about moving. The only way you're going to turn the frightening unknown into the comfortable familiar is by getting out of your house and seeing what's out there. Walk the streets. See the sights. Meet people.

Sitting in your house is just going to prolong your discomfort, give you time to brood and make you bored.

11. Get away from your spouse. Your husband/wife or boyfriend/girlfriend (if you bring one) is going to be your greatest source of support as well as misery. I heard somewhere that 50% of marriages end when moving to a new country. I don't know if that's true, but I can guarantee you that moving to a new country is one of the greatest challenges your relationship will ever face. In order for your relationship (as well as the trip itself) to work you're going to need to have patience with one another, communicate with one another, compromise with one another and spend some time away from one another. Even if it's just a walk in the park, you're going to need to get away from your significant other on a regular basis to clear the air and not get on each other's nerves.

12. Start a blog. Writing a blog is a great way to stay in touch with family and friends, express your thoughts and offer advice you wish you would have been given about things you had to learn the hard way. In addition to that, it's a rewarding experience. It adds another level to your adventure and provides you with a digital scrapbook to look back on. Just make sure to set it up before you leave home so you don't have to stress about setting it up when you're in country dealing with a thousand other things.

NORTH ISLAND VS SOUTH ISLAND

New Zealand is made up of two islands: the North Island and the South Island. Actually, there are thousands of 1-3 acre islands all along the coasts, but most of those are wildlife preserves you can't go to. So for all practical purposes, New Zealand is made up of two islands separated by 90 kilometers of angry ocean. If you're planning on moving to New Zealand you're going to have to pick which island you want to move to. Neither island is objectively better or worse than the other. Which island you should move to depends on what kind of lifestyle you're looking for and more importantly, where you can find a job. Having said that, there are some differences between the North and South worth talking about, but it's hard to point out those differences without making overgeneralizations that someone might find exception and take offense to. Lucky for you, I'm going to go ahead and make those overgeneralizations anyway to help familiarize you with New Zealand.

The difference between the North and South island stem mainly from the fact that Auckland is on the North Island. That alone puts 1/3 of the country's population in the North Island. Auckland is also the country's main point of entry for goods, people and money. Even though Wellington (which is also on the North Island) is the political capital of New Zealand, Auckland is functionally the center of New Zealand. The farther away from Auckland you get the less money there is. The less money there is the less infrastructure there is. The less infrastructure there is the lower the quality of life is by material standards; towns have fewer stores, and the stores stock fewer products...and the internet connectivity is much worse.

This phenomenon is as true in Texas as it is in New Zealand. The world is divided into big cities and backwoods with degrees in between them. New Zealand is already relatively disconnected from the rest of the world by the fact that it's at the bottom of the world. The South island is a little more disconnected since it's geographically separated from Auckland. Granted, it still has big cities, airports and maritime ports that bring in a constant stream of goods, people and money, but it *feels* more disconnected from the rest of the world. You feel like you're taking a step back in time when you go there. If the South island looked like West Texas this would be a bad thing, but the effect is more romantic since the South island looks like paradise.

As many modern conveniences as Auckland has there are a lot of Kiwis who would never live there and who say that Auckland isn't "the real New Zealand." If there is such a thing as "the real New Zealand" then it must be the South island. The South island is just absurdly beautiful, tranquil and homespun. It would be the most visited, most celebrated paradise on earth if it weren't for the apocalyptic swarms of mosquitoes and the arctic cold ocean water.

This isn't to say that the North Island is ugly. It's got plenty of scenery that's so amazing a photo can't do it justice, and it's certainly got the most inviting hot springs and beaches in the country, but the South island has more mountains, waterfalls, glaciers, lakes, seals, penguins and fjords. Traveling around the North Island is likely to make you think, "Man, I'd really like to live here." Traveling around the South island is likely to make you think, "Man, I never want to leave here." But you will have to leave because even if you had a visa you'd have a harder time finding a job on the South Island than you would on the North Island.

That's the difference between the North and South islands in a nutshell, but the issue is more complicated than that because each island is made up of its own diverse sub-regions, which I'll explain to you. The maps below were divided up by me. They don't necessarily represent states or provinces. It's mainly just how I see New Zealand.

Everything not included in a box on both of the maps below are either empty farmland, national parks or cities so isolated by farmlands and national parks that they don't constitute a major, unique region. That and/or I haven't been there and don't know enough about the place to describe it.

Now let's take a look at the North Island.

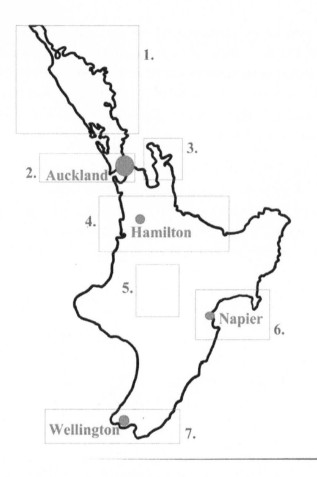

1. This area is known as "The North Land." I didn't make that up. This area is full of rolling hills, sheep farms, gentle beaches, small towns and old white people. It doesn't have majestic peaks or a wild nightlife.

2. Auckland is a region in and of itself. It's a major city with 1.4 million people. Auckland has the largest concentration of Pacific Islanders in the world. It's very culturally diverse, but at the same time, it suffers a little from the soullessness that comes with sprawling suburbs and office buildings.

3. The Coromandel Peninsula is where Aucklanders go for spring break. There are a lot of good beaches but not a lot of jobs.

4. This is where the Shire was filmed in "The Lord of the Rings." You can think of this whole area as the Shire with its small towns and cozy green hills. You can also think of the city of Hamilton as Mordor….because it's a shit box.

5. Lake Taupo is picturesque and has tons of adventure sports. Just South of Lake Taupo are two large mountains where you can go hiking, camping and skiing. There's a lot of big adventure here, and in order to be ordained a true Kiwi you have to hike the Tongariro Crossing.

6. Hawkes Bay is warm and breezy. It has a lot of orchards and vineyards, which means it has a lot of rich farmers. It also has a lot of poor farm hands who are addicted to meth. Hawkes Bay also has a really high unemployment rate. Flaxmere is the stabbing capital of New Zealand.

7. Ever been to Oregon or Washington State? Then you've been to the Southern tip of the North Island. It's cold, rainy and liberal.

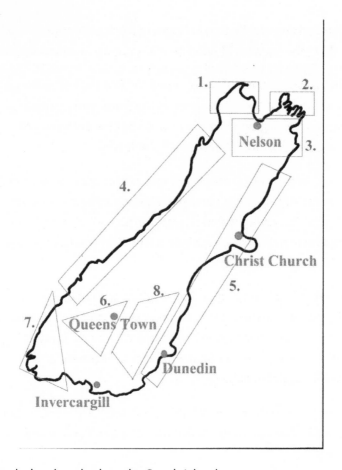

Now let's take a look at the South Island.

1. The Abel Tasman Peninsula is mostly rugged national park. It's got great views and good weather. It's isolated and full of hippies.

2. The Marlborough Sounds are the perfect place to ride out the apocalypse. It's a giant mash of peninsulas as crooked as the devil's backbone. This means it takes a lot of gas to get nowhere, but 1 square kilometer of property could have 3 kilometers of coastline.

3. This is wine country....if you're into that kind of thing. This area has the best weather in New Zealand, and it's where the ferries between the North and South islands dock. So it's pretty well connected to the world. This is where I want to move some day, and you should to.

4. There's not much civilization on the West coast, but the scenery is very memorable.

5. Most of the South Island's population resides along the East coast. There are a lot of great beach towns like Kaikoura. It's also got the big towns like Christchurch and Dunedin. If you want to move to the South island then start at the top of the East coast and drive south dropping off job applications in every town along the way.

6. This is lake country. It's spectacularly beautiful. In a country full of picturesque views, the locals come here for the views.

7. This is Fjordland National Park. It's the most beautiful place in New Zealand. People who live in lake country come here for the views. It's pretty cold and remote though. Young children would probably be happier in Nelson, but if you want to escape the world and get back to nature then pick one of the towns on the edge of the fjordlands like Manapouri or Te Anau.

8. This is the Otago region. Most of the South Island is made up of rugged, beautiful mountains, but Otago is an oasis of rolling hills. The whole area has an aura of peacefulness around it. It's just far enough away from the world to feel left alone but close enough get what you want.

If you want to completely disappear from the world then pick one of the tiny towns in the middle of the South Island where I didn't draw a box. Also, I didn't draw a box around Invercargill because you don't want to move there.

There's a large island south of the South Island called Stewart Island, but it's a bird sanctuary. So unless you're a park ranger you're probably not going to be able to live there.

WHAT'S THE BEST CITY IN NEW ZEALAND?

There's no best city in New Zealand to live in. The question is, which city best suits you? Having said that, the city that offers you a job is (initially) the best city in New Zealand, and since one-third of New Zealand's population lives in and around Auckland that means one-third of the jobs are in Auckland. So Auckland is the most obvious choice of cities to move to. However, if you're moving to New Zealand to escape the daily grind and get back to nature then moving to a city of 1.4 million people defeats the purpose.

A quick glance at a map of New Zealand will show thousands of cities to choose from and make you feel overwhelmed. However, most of those cities have less than 20,000 people in them and only a few jobs, which you'll probably have to wait for someone to die to get. Even then, the job will probably go to someone who is on a first name basis with the prospective employer. If you look at the list of cities in New Zealand with more than 20,000 people the list becomes much more manageable. I'll go through that list and tell you what I can of each city. However, bear in mind that this is only one person's opinions, and they're based on his limited experiences. I've also only included cities that I've been to. So I've left a few off, but if they weren't impressive enough to draw me to them then that must say something.

Christchurch (Pop 360,000) Christchurch is built on relatively flat land, which means is has relatively straight roads (a rare luxury in New Zealand). The geography of the city allows business and subdivisions plenty of room to build. Immediately outside the city limits, you'll find rolling hills and picturesque beaches favored by people, seals, penguins and dolphins. I was put off by

Christchurch a little because it reminded me too much of America with its strip malls and intersections. However, the locals swear by it, and if you're worried about culture shock then the easy navigability of this city will help ease you into your new life.

The downside of Christchurch is that it has been hit by a series of earthquakes recently, and nobody knows if there will be more. As a result, people are leaving the city in droves and heading to Dunedin. This means the city is losing jobs, but housing prices are dropping, and the businesses that remain are desperate for employees.

Wellington (Pop 200,000) and Lower Hutt (Pop 100,000) If you like Seattle you'll like Wellington and its sister city, Lower Hutt. The weather is notoriously bad. It's cold, windy and rainy. However, the city has a vibrant indie feel to it. The main tourist street downtown (comparable to New Orleans' Bourbon Street or Austin's 6th Street) is called "Cuba St." This anti-establishment, left-wing title is echoed in the city's counter culture. The architecture is vibrant, and the surrounding mountains offer plenty of houses with a view (though usually the view is of dark clouds).

Hamilton (Pop 145,000) Like Christchurch, Hamilton has unusually flat land that is conducive to business. However, the city lacks impressive architecture and generally has a grimy Detroit feel to it. If I were a meth head I would move to Hamilton, but I'm not. So it would take a damned good job offer to lure me to Hamilton, especially when there are so many more spectacular cities in New Zealand.

Dunedin (Pop 118,000) The weather isn't perfect, but the architecture is stunning. Unfortunately, a lot of its Victorian mansions have been turned into slums for university students. Speaking of which, Dunedin is New Zealand's quintessential university town. This makes it lots of fun for young people, but if celebrating the new year by burning couches in the streets isn't your thing you may not want to settle down here. Also, when the university students are gone for summer break the population that's left seems to be mainly red necks and geriatrics.

Hastings (Pop 75,000) and Napier (Pop 57,000) The Hawkes bay area where Hastings and Napier are located enjoys unusually good weather, and as such boasts a number of wineries. Napier is famous for its art deco architecture, but in my opinion, they overplayed that card a little. Napier is a posh area that would be good to raise kids in, but young adults looking for a trendy scene would do better in Nelson, Wellington or Dunedin. Hastings is a farming community with a high unemployment rate. Unless you're a farmer I would not suggest moving to Hastings.

Rotorua (Pop 69,000) Rotorua's foresighted city council has gone to great lengths to turn the city into a tourism mecca. There are hot springs and geothermal activity that make the area a geologist's heaven. However, active sulfur vents make the town smell like rotten egg fart most of the year. You get used to it in a day or two and don't notice it anymore, but you still live in a town famous for smelling like rotten egg fart. Having said that, if other people don't want to work there then there may be a job opening for you.

Invercargill (Pop 53,000) This town is located at the southernmost tip of New Zealand. This means Invercargill has two major setbacks: isolation and arctic weather. The downtown area has some beautiful architecture, but the whole town has a cloud of dejection hanging over it. It's like so many isolated American red neck towns in the dirty south that all the young people want to escape from but never do. Point in fact; the most famous person from Invercargill was a womanizing, suicidal mechanic. Most Kiwis I've spoken to have advised against moving to Invercargill.

Nelson (Pop 46,000) At the northern most tip of the south island, Nelson enjoys the best weather in New Zealand. The downtown area doesn't have the most awe-inspiring architecture, but it's laid out well. Plus, it's got plenty of coast, and it's a short drive to some of the most beautiful scenery in New Zealand. Most Kiwis I've spoken to have recommended moving to Nelson, and after spending a few days there I agree with them.

Timaru (Pop 45,000) Timaru is big but quiet. I was impressed by its sleepy, peaceful vibe, but younger immigrants may find it a bit dull.

Taupo (Pop 34,000) Taupo is a favorite tourist destination for Kiwis. It's got plenty of tourist attractions, a beautiful lake, and it claims to be the skydiving capital of the world. You would not regret moving to Taupo.

Blenheim (Pop 30,000) You can tell which regions in New Zealand have the best weather by the number of wineries they have, and Blenheim has wineries on every corner. If you're the kind of person who likes the kind of people who like wineries then give Blenheim a good, hard look.

Queenstown (Pop 29,000) Queenstown is the quintessential tourist trap. A breathtaking lake nestled between prime skiing and hiking mountains makes this a favorite tourist destination for Kiwis. Some people complain that it's over-commercialized, but it's over-commercialized because so many people want to go there. The only problem is that since tourism is its main industry you'll have trouble finding work in practically any other field.

Tauranga (Pop 115,000) Tauranga bills itself as "the Florida of New Zealand." It just doesn't mention that the part of Florida it's most like is the part with all the retirement homes. Tauranga is a lovely town with a nice beach and a nice downtown area. Somehow there's just not much to do there. If you want to wind down the clock painting the sunset, Tauranga is for you. If you're looking for a beach town with a faster pulse, then head down to Nelson.

Two cities that didn't make the list because I've never been there are New Plymouth (Pop 70,000), which I know nothing about, and Palmerston North (Pop. 82,000), which has been voted the worst city in New Zealand and John Cleese [from Monty Python] once referred to as the best city to kill yourself in.

INTRO TO SMALL TOWN NEW ZEALAND

These are just a few small towns we've visited in New Zealand that particularly stood out to us. If you don't move to any of these towns, they're at least worth visiting if you take a road trip around New Zealand.

Oamaru (Population 13,000) Oamaru was a booming port city a century ago before a storm destroyed its port and all the major industries went bust. During its heyday, the town sprouted a magnificent Victorian downtown area and neighborhoods full of enormous Victorian houses that you can now buy for a fraction of the cost you'd pay just about anywhere else in New Zealand. If you're not impressed by the city's architecture the two penguin colonies will definitely steal your heart. The city needs to fire its politicians and hire the people responsible for making Rotorua an international tourist destination. I predict that in a few decades Oamaru will finally get the attention it deserves from tourists and industries, and when that happens you'll wish you'd bought some of the cheap property they're practically giving away there now.

Kaikoura (Population 2,200) Kaikoura is damn near the perfect beach town. It's got views of seal colonies on one side and awe-inspiring views of the mountains on the other. The main strip runs right along the beach and has all the restaurants, bars and beachwear shops you need. Go to Kaikoura. Go.

Hanmer Springs (Population 800) This cozy town is nestled among the evergreens high in the central mountains of the South Island and boasts a very posh thermal hot pool resort. This is where the rich go to relax and boost the property value. Like Oamaru, 20 years from now you'll really wish you'd bought property here when there was still undeveloped land to be bought.

Arrow Town (Population 2,100) Arrow Town is an old gold-mining town that exploits the hell out of its roots for the sake of tourism. It feels like an Old West American gold mining town except for all the Jade stores selling Maori-inspired jewelry. The town is quaint and peaceful, and it's a short drive to famous Queenstown.

Gore (Population 12,000) Other than for trout fishing, there's no reason to go to Gore.

Greymouth (Population 13,000) There's nothing exceptional about the city of Greymouth, but it makes the list because it's the largest city on the west side of the south island, which is one of the most beautiful parts of New Zealand. So Greymouth is sort of like an outpost town on the edge of a wild and beautiful frontier. If you're coming to New Zealand for adventure then Greymouth may be a good home base for you.

Takaka (Population 1,200) Takaka is located in the ridiculously beautiful Able Tasman Peninsula. Cut off from the rest of the world by a long, winding mountainous road, Takaka has become a favored destination of hippies looking for an out-of-the-way place to sell handmade art, go rock climbing and smoke weed.

Ohakune (Population 1,200) Ohakune is your quintessential ski resort town. So if that's what you're looking for, this is where you'll find it.

Raglan (Population 2,600) Raglan is the quintessential surfer town. So if that's what you're looking for, this is where you'll find it.

Waiheke Island (Population 7,600) Waiheke Island is just a short ferry ride from Auckland. The commute could be expensive if you plan on working in Auckland, but there are some jobs on the island itself, and once you go there you might not want to leave. It's got all the beaches and wineries you need, and if there's ever a zombie apocalypse you'd be hard-pressed to find a more secure and comfortable haven.

Warkworth (Population 3200) Warkworth is a great all-around small town. It's got a charming and bustling downtown area that wraps around a sleepy river. It's also a short drive to some seriously awesome beaches like Goat Island. It's not too far from Auckland if you ever get the hankering for the big city, and you can stop at Snow Planet to do some indoor skiing on the way.

WHAT SHOULD YOU BRING WITH YOU WHEN MOVING TO NEW ZEALAND?

One of the first issues you have to deal with when moving to a foreign country is the question of what stuff you should bring with you, what stuff you should ship and what stuff you should sell.

You already know what you're going to pack in your carry-on luggage: clothes, portable electronics and maybe a few knickknacks with sentimental value. What you do with the rest of your stuff depends on one factor: money. Shipping anything to New Zealand is incredibly expensive. Shipping a box of blankets from the U.S.A. to New Zealand could easily run you over $100.

The simplest solution to the moving issue is to sell everything you don't need and rebuy everything when you get to New Zealand. However, the downside to this strategy is that buying new stuff can be as expensive as shipping it from overseas, and moving to a new country is stressful enough without running all over town stocking your house with all the stuff you take for granted like a college freshman who just left home and realized for the first time that if you don't go to the store and buy toothpaste you won't have any.

If you're rich I would advise putting all your household goods in a shipping container and have it sent via freighter. It'll take a few months to get to you, but it'll take you a few months to get settled in anyway. Oh, and pets cost about $1,000 to ship from the U.S.A. to NZ, and they have to be kept in quarantine for about 6 months (if they're eligible at all [snakes and spiders are not]).

When you actually fly to New Zealand don't bring any toiletries on the plane with you. You can buy all that stuff cheaply at your local Countdown (which will, by the way, deliver your groceries to your house for a very small fee) or Warehouse. Use the extra room in your luggage to pack your lucky hat or sock money beer koozie. And wear your heaviest, bulkiest clothes on the airplane and fill all the pockets with stuff. A bomber jacket or a pair of heavy duty work boots can take up half the space and weight limit on your luggage, but if it's on your back or your feet you won't be penalized for it or have to pay to ship it.

You will most likely be able to use your current cell phone in New Zealand. You'll just need to replace the SIM chip though you may have to jump through a few more hoops if you have a smartphone. You can pick up a SIM chip at a Countdown or any cell phone store, which you can find in most town centers or the mall. Be aware that you'll need to buy a power converter for any 110 volt electronics you have because New Zealand uses 220 volt. Most laptops are dual voltage. So you'll only need a converter for the shape of the plug. For other electronic devices, you'll need an actual power converter, which is expensive, a pain in the butt and will probably fry your electronic device in the long run anyway. I would not advise bringing stuff like an electric beard trimmer or a fancy alarm clock. Just buy a new one with the right plug and the right voltage when you get to New Zealand.

You'll also want to buy a street map as soon as arrive in New Zealand. If you can afford it, I would strongly recommend getting a GPS device. In fact, I would insist that you buy a GPS device. It will save you sooooo much heartache in the long run. The roads in most of New Zealand's major cities aren't built on a grid system or any other logical, intuitive pattern. So any help you can get navigating the country will lower your stress level.

If you're on a budget then the best place to get household items is TradeMe, which is the New Zealand equivalent of EBay or Craigslist. You can actually find just about anything on TradeMe. In fact, you will use TradeMe eventually. So you may as well go ahead and get acquainted with it.

SO YOU'RE MOVING TO AUCKLAND, WHAT YOU SHOULD KNOW

The first thing you need to understand about Auckland is that the city doesn't stop at the city line. It's like Los Angeles where the city sprawl has grown so big that you can drive through 4 cities and think they're all one city because the buildings just run together all the way across. The actual city, what you will come to see as Auckland if you live here, is a giant blob that's shaped like a stack of runny eggs spilling down from Auckland's North Shore to Papakura. So when you go job hunting don't assume that all the jobs are directly at the little point on the map specifically labeled "Auckland." See the rest of the streets on the map? Those other streets have jobs too.

Looking at a map of Auckland you're likely to get fixated on the CBD (central business district), which is the area around Queens Street. On a map, it looks like Auckland revolves around this area. This isn't necessarily true. It would be more correct to call the central business district the North Eastern professional business district. Here's why.

The CBD is where the Sky Tower, most of the universities, a few high-rise office buildings, most of the real expensive hotels, the fancy nightlife, red light district, yacht harbor and tourist shopping are at. It's like downtown New York...except without the constant fear of imminent death and rude taxi drivers.

There are a lot of jobs in the CBD, but they're mainly high paid professional office jobs and minimum wage retail service jobs. If your skills don't have you standing behind a cash register or sitting in an office cubicle then you might not want to focus your housing and job searching in and around the CBD. I'm not saying don't look there. Just, expand your search really far away as well.

I want to say a few more things about the CBD, because you will go there eventually. The CBD has several major roads you should know about. Queen Street is the main street, but running perpendicular across the south end of Queen St. is Karangahape Road. Don't worry if you can't pronounce that. Most locals can't either. So everyone calls it "K. Road." That's the red light district, and everything about it is dilapidated. Head north down K Road for a kilometer or two and you'll run into Ponsonby. Ponsonby is a microcosm of Austin, TX. It used to be the bohemian place off the beaten track, but when the business district grew over the backstreet, the back street sold out. Now it's an over-commercialized den of upper middle-class young people pretending to be hip. Don't get me wrong. There are some nice clubs and shops on Ponsonby. Just wait to go there until you have a lot of extra spending money. And dress nice to avoid condescending looks of disapproval.

If you head due east from Queen St. for about two kilometers you'll cross a bunch of college campuses and a couple of parks (that are all completely safe to walk in) and find New Market. It wouldn't be incorrect to call New Market a strip mall, but it's really something more. It's a long street lined (on both sides) with all the stores you'd find in a quality mall. Scattered randomly between the shops are chain and ethnic restaurants. It's a good place to go if you're looking to buy overpriced designer clothes for an interview.

So the CBD is shaped like a pitchfork with Ponsonby, Queen St. And New Market making up the points and K Road is the bar on the bottom connecting them. Once you leave that pitchfork area you start getting into suburbia. However, this is suburbia on acid. Auckland is a melting pot of architecture. Most of the houses were designed by early British expat frontier folk who built these massive frontier farm houses with solid wood floors and long hallways. (You'll probably end up sharing a flat with 5 other adults in one of these giant houses). Then they covered them in Victorian style awnings, windows, porches and roofs. Eventually, the city grew over the farm houses. Apparently, art deco architecture was all the rage back then, because now you'll find leaky faux adobe/pueblo-style homes all over the place. You can tell which houses were built in the 80s, because they look like the cars from back then: faded pastel colors, broad and box shaped with boring window shapes. Then the modern Euro trend took off in Auckland. A lot of old buildings have been torn down and replaced with minimalist shipping container houses with hipster angles and frosted glass everywhere. There aren't a lot of apartment complexes in Auckland because of the potential to be knocked down by earthquakes.

Auckland's haphazard architectural style is made more spastic by the area's geography. Imagine if 12 volcanoes just popped up in the middle of Los Angeles and warped all the ground between them so that now there are hills everywhere. That's Auckland. There's not a straight road in the whole damn town. Everything curves around something. This means half the houses have amazing views, but the other half lost their view of the sky.

Speaking of the sky, it rains most of the year, which nourishes the already nutrient-rich volcanic rock so that every seed that hits the ground bursts forth vibrantly to life. Now giant elephant ear plants, palm trees and every oversized tropical flower you can imagine are exploding out of the fences of every yard in suburbia. Now squeeze in over 800 parks, and that's what Auckland looks like.

But it gets weirder. Somewhat randomly throughout the surrounding sprawl, you'll find mini-main streets of varying sizes. These are smaller, poorer, more ethnic, more local versions of Ponsonby, Queen Street and New Market. St. Lukes is large and highly commercialized. Onehunga's strip is large and very local. There are no clubs on Mount Eden's main street, but there is in Elerslie. Other towns like Mangere Bridge have short streets with token establishments: a dairy (aka cramped, dusty convenience store run by Indians, Arabs and Asians), a Turkish Kebab restaurant with one table, an awesome fish and chips hole in the wall, 4 places to get coffee, a tiny liquor store with terrible hours, an Asian vegetable shop, a pharmacy and one out-of-place business like a vacuum cleaner store or real estate office. These main street areas always have awnings over the footpaths (aka sidewalks) plastered with old, faded ice cream ads.

No matter where you live in the greater Auckland area you'll probably live within walking distance of at least one of these mini main streets, and that's part of the charm of living in Auckland: walking down to your town center for a coffee or driving around town aimlessly trying to find a new main street with some hidden gem of a restaurant or novelty store.

This suburban sprawl radiates east from the CBD until it hits the ocean and south until it hits Manukau. Even the people who live here can't agree how to pronounce "Manukau." Radio commercials always pronounce it "Monico," but in conversation, I always hear people pronounce it, "Manicow." Manukau is a second CBD that's more industrial and not touristy. The rent is cheaper there than around the Queen Street CBD, and you'll probably have more housing options. However, the farther south you go the more likely you are to be accosted by a meth head. From what I understand, Papakura and Mangere Township are two of the most dangerous places to live. They're not Compton by any stretch of the imagination, but still not the first choice for frail, pasty white people.

Manukau has lots of blue collar jobs and decent neighborhoods around it. A lot of the big industrial stores are there. So if you know you're going to be buying a lot of widgets for your business you should plan on doing a lot of shopping in and around Manukau.

Right outside the airport is the industrial area. If you do warehouse work there's a good chance you'll end up there. If you're anyone else, you don't need to be there. Don't reserve a hotel just outside the airport for the first week you live in Auckland. You'll be staring at warehouses, parking lots and trucker food restaurants wondering why you moved to a post-apocalyptic country.

The three most important factors you need to consider when picking your first house or hostel in Auckland is food, shopping and transportation. You're going to have to go grocery shopping all the time. The farther away you are from a grocery store the more exhausting, daunting and expensive your life will be. Countdown is the big grocery store chain. Look for housing close to one. You can also do your shopping online and have your groceries delivered from Countdown for a small fee. Pack N' Save is a failed attempt at imitating Costco or Sam's Club. You can do your shopping there, but the selection is bad, and I never noticed much of a savings buying in bulk there. Meat at Pack N' Save is cheaper than Countdown though.

In addition to food, you're also going to need towels, silverware, bed lamps, pillows, blankets, underwear, chairs and every other little thing that fills up a house. You'll need to buy a lot of basics first, and you won't realize what you need all at once. So you're going to have to make regular trips to some place where you can get all this stuff. You can wander around every main street in Auckland looking for enough random shops to fill all your shopping needs or you can just go the Warehouse. The Warehouse's selection sucks, but it will serve a vital role in your life nonetheless, and the closer you can position yourself to one the less painful and inconvenienced your domestic life will be. If you want to do some super, super cheap shopping immediately after arriving in New Zealand you should check out one of the farmer's markets and the Mangere Township weekend market (not to be confused with the Mangere Bridge weekend market). Look them up on the internet for more details. You can just catch a bus to either of those though. You don't need to live next door.

The last thing you'll need is transportation. If you don't take anything else into consideration, look at the bus and train lines running through Auckland and get close to one of them. You'll find them at www.maxx.co.nz. The public transportation system in Auckland isn't the best in the world, but that's the worst thing I can say about it. It's simple to use. It's clean. It's safe. It's respectable. The better you understand it and the more you use it the easier your life will be. Be aware that buses won't stop for you unless you wave them down.

When it comes time to buy a car you have 3 options. If you've got more money than time you can do a Google search for car dealerships and take a taxi to one. If you moved to New Zealand with less than $30,000 to your name you can take the bus to the Elerslie Car Fair any weekend and haggle with a local. Just make sure to get there early. That's how we bought our first New Zealand car.

You'll find the biggest selection of the cheapest cars on www.trademe.co.nz. That's also a great place to buy home furnishings. The site works just like EBay. If you can't figure out how to use it you shouldn't be moving to a foreign country, especially New Zealand since TradeMe should be the first place you look for a job too.

Having said all that, here's a rundown on Auckland's towns starting on the North side of town going South:

The North Shore- If you take Highway 1 over the harbor it'll take you to Northcote Point. This area and everything around Takapuna, Hauraki, Baywater, Devonport is a really nice place to live, but it's expensive, and the traffic over the harbor bridge is terrible during the morning and afternoon commute.

Waitakere/Swanson- Rich people houses.

Glen Eden/New Lynn- Has a reputation for being a bad neighborhood, and it's proud of its reputation.

Hillsborough- Nice neighborhood with good access to the highway and bus routes. Rent is a little high, but it's not the worst. This is a good place for established professional working couples to raise a family.

Grey Lynn/St. Lukes- An okay area. It's close to the nightlife and a lot of shops, but traffic is going to be a big part of your life.

Mount Eden/Three Kings- Everything down Mount Eden Road is nice. It's not the highest class side of town, but it's a good all-around place to live. If you can't figure out where to live, start here.

One Tree Hill- Kind of a rich neighborhood.

Onehunga- You could say it's kind of lower class, but it's got character, and it's conveniently located.

Oranga- This is a shitty neighborhood.

Remuera/Mission Bay/Botany Downs- Very nice neighborhoods. Bankers live here.

Ellerslie/Mount Wellington- There's nice parts and bad parts. It depends what street you live on.

Mangare Bridge- Quaint area. Nice water front. It's not the nicest side of town, but it's affordable without being true ghetto.

Mangare/Mangare East/Favona/Papatoetoe/East Tamaki- This is the ghetto. Don't move there.

Manukau- This is your standard concrete city. There are lots of jobs in Maukau and lots to do. There's also traffic and noise, but you might be into that.

THE HOUSING MARKET IN NEW ZEALAND

We have a lot of good things to say about living in New Zealand, but the housing market isn't one of them.

Buying: The difficulty in buying property in New Zealand starts with finding property. In America, they have a nationwide MLS (multiple listing service) that has almost every property for sale and can be accessed from millions of different real estate websites. So it's easy to find out what's available anywhere. The New Zealand system is much more fractured. You have to find the real estate agents in the area you're interested in and contact them individually.

Luckily there aren't many real estate agencies in New Zealand, and you can generally head to any downtown area and easily find their offices where they'll have print outs of their properties taped to the windows for pedestrians to peruse. We recently drove the length of New Zealand and made a point of studying the window listings in every town we stopped in to find out where the cheapest properties are.

The survey wasn't encouraging. In America, you can find "fixer-uppers" for as little as $30,000 in most cities, and there are rural areas where bare land sells for as low as $1,000 per acre. Obviously, it's not the best land...in fact, it's the worst, but it is an option. Super low-cost property like that is practically non-existent in New Zealand. In our informal, unprofessional survey of New Zealand property, we couldn't find any houses or even bare land for less than $80,000 even in small towns. I'm sure they're out there somewhere, but they're few and far between.

If you're looking for property, you can generally expect a starting price of $150,000, but the average advertised price seems to be around $400,000. Oddly, this seems to be true regardless of the size of town you're looking at. Of course, if you're a millionaire then the sky is the limit; you'll be able to get a mansion overlooking majestic coastlines. You can even get your own winery. New Zealand is a great place for millionaires.

You can always build your own house, but be aware that there's very little flat land in New Zealand. So there's a good chance your cost of building will have to include leveling part of a hill and possibly installing your own rainwater collection system and septic tank. And since New Zealand is an island you'll likely have to buy imported materials, and there's not a lot of competing businesses to drive the price down.

Building your own home can be an attractive option because many houses in New Zealand were built in postcolonial days when building codes were much slimmer. There are a lot of cold, leaky houses in New Zealand...with gorgeous hardwood floors and elegant Victorian facades. As pretty as they are on the outside, New Zealand really should tear down most of its houses and rebuild them correctly.

I will say this on a positive note. Old New Zealand houses have character. There aren't many bland, Edward Scissor Hands cookie-cutter suburbs, and since a lot of the houses were built in postcolonial days when large families were the norm, houses tend to be really big. Unfortunately, this drives the price up. A lot of the new houses are built in a futuristic, minimalist, cubist Euro style, which is refreshingly stylistic, but again, you pay for style.

Financing your home is going to be difficult. New Zealand isn't big on credit. I don't know the average interest rate you'll have to pay, but I do know you can expect to have to put down a 20%

down payment on your property. On the upside, there aren't 1 million different banks and convoluted finance institutions offering a dizzying array of options for financing your house. This means the process of financing will be a little more straightforward, but it also means there's not as much competition driving the price down either.

One thing that is confusing and dizzying about buying property in New Zealand is that half the properties are sold at auction or "by negotiation." So it's extremely difficult to figure out the true cost of property in any given area. I guess you just have to talk to a real estate agent to navigate the invisible maze of auction costs.

Renting: Since buying real estate in New Zealand is so expensive most people rent, which is unreasonably complicated and expensive as well. The best place to find rental properties is on Trademe.co.nz. At least that's simple, but expect to have to fill out an application to even be considered to rent a property. The application often asks for references, proof of employment and a credit check. This complicates things if you're a newly arrived immigrant with no local references, but your property manager is likely to understand the situation you're in and may actually contact your overseas reference. So be sure to bring that contact information with you when you immigrate.

If you're living in Auckland then you can expect to pay a minimum of $100 per week, and most properties rent by the week, not by the month. It's hit or miss whether or not your rent covers utilities, and you can expect to share the house with several other people. We currently share a house with two other people. Last year we shared a house with five other people. If you want your own home you can expect to pay $300-$500 per week.

FINDING A RENTAL PROPERTY

NZ is amazing. The cities offer an awesome array of culture and free entertainment. Rural NZ, which is most of the country, is covered by lush, green rolling hills and deserted beaches. I've never regretted my move to NZ from the US... until my landlord told me he was going to sell the house we were renting. Only then was I exposed to the Dark Side of NZ. Over the next two months, I questioned my own worth and the integrity of NZ's property managers as a whole.

General Observations during my search:

• Property Managers hold no qualms about lying in ads. 'Three double bedrooms" usually means one double bedroom, one bedroom that will fit a double bed as long as you don't expect to open the closet door, and the third bedroom is really a larger than normal hall closet that might fit a crib and a chair if you're lucky. Just don't close the door, because I wouldn't trust the oxygen to hold out for more than a few minutes.

• Pictures lie. Trademe.co.nz is the main place to find rentals throughout NZ. If the property manager puts an ounce of effort into the ad it can be very helpful; rent, bond, pet situation, address, etc. There is also a place to put pictures of the property. Quoting an article I found during the worst moments of my search:

"You absolutely cannot rely on photos made by the rental agency (this also applies to buying houses for that matter). I have never seen as skillful a photographer as the Kiwi real estate agent. Misleading is the only correct word for it. The house in the picture looks great, but you can't see the garbage dump in the garden, the sky blue kitchen with a 20-year-old electric stove with only one element in working order, or the neighboring deteriorated back street houses. "

• The general rental property under NZ$600 a week will have many, if not most of the issues below:

• Mold, if you can't see it you will smell it

• Peeling Paint/wallpaper

• Carpet that my dead Grandmother would find shockingly tacky

• No insulation

• Several houses had someone living below it. This would have been something important to mention in the ad!

I had one property manager that had never seen the property before and was unable to explain what was behind the locked door at the bottom of the stairs. His guess was maybe someone lived there. Or aliens, whatever. Several showed up the 30 minute showing late or not at all. Thank you I really had nothing better to do at 1pm on a Tuesday, it's not like I took off work for this or anything! There was one ad that read "Open house Monday at 12noon for ten minutes. This will be the ONLY showing." What the hell, I want your job!

The whole experience of looking at rentals highlighted the downside to a society of relaxed and otherwise flexible people. I've learned I don't want a relaxed, flexible landlord. I would prefer someone that fixes things when they break and addresses issues before they become a health problem. I spent two months looking at houses I really didn't want to live in, but of course applied for every one of them.

In the end, we found a lovely three bedroom house that's managed by the owner, not an agency. How did we snatch up this diamond in the rough? We weren't able to see the inside of the house before we agreed to sign a lease. It was that or be homeless.

SURVINGING IN NEW ZEALAND ON A BUDGET

There's nothing I'm going to say here that you wouldn't figure out on your after living in New Zealand for three months, but the less you have to figure out on your own the first hectic three months of living in a foreign country the better.

Probably the biggest downside of living in New Zealand is the cost of living. The housing market in New Zealand is a complete train wreck, and consumer goods are excessively expensive because so many of them have to be shipped in from overseas at great expense, and a lot of the consumer goods that are produced locally get shipped out overseas where they can be sold for a bigger profit. The scarcity that creates in New Zealand means locally made products that are sold locally can be sold at a higher price. What can I say? Businesses are greedy everywhere in the world. Such is life.

The first thing you're going to need to do when you arrive in New Zealand is to find housing. To do that, go to http://www.trademe.co.nz/flatmates-wanted and find a house with three strangers living in it who are renting out their fourth spare bedroom. That's how it's done in New Zealand. If you want a place of your own you had better sell a child before you get here. Your other option is living out of a camper van, which is a surprisingly popular choice for tourists.

Trademe.co.nz is also a great place to find free or cheap furniture and all the random, weird stuff you need. We just bought a cat tree off of TradeMe today. That's also where you'll want to go to look for jobs. It's Craigslist and EBay rolled into one. I've said it before, and I'll say it again. If you live in New Zealand long enough you're going to use TradeMe eventually.

There are a few tricks to grocery shopping that can lower your food budget. There are only a few big grocery stores in New Zealand: "Countdown" and "New World." If you shop at a small town grocery store you're probably paying too much for your food. If you shop at Countdown and don't get a "One Card" you'll miss out on vital discounts when shopping at Countdown.

The third big grocery store in New Zealand is "Pack N Save," which offers less variety than the other big grocery stores, but it sells in bulk at a discount. However, if you do all your grocery shopping at Pack N Save you probably won't actually save any money; you have to do selective shopping to make it worth your while.

Speaking of selective shopping, New Zealand has a lot of weekend farmer's markets, fruits and vegetable specialty stores and butcher shops. If you have more free time than money you should definitely look into doing your meat and vegetable shopping at these specialty shops. You'll get plumper products at a cheaper price, but the real savings at the butcher shops comes from buying in bulk. So if you don't have a big freezer then the butcher shop might not be worth it.

If you're really hardcore about saving money you can go surfcasting fishing and catch your own dinner. We went camping once and watched a teen fish all morning long. Then he came by each of the camp sites and offered to sell everyone the fish he caught. I suppose you could even supplement your income that way. You don't need a fishing license, but there are very strict limits on what you can catch and how much.

For all your household shopping needs there's "The Warehouse." That's pretty much the only store comparable to Wal~Mart. So when you find out which New Zealand city you're going to live in, figure out where its Warehouse is, because you're going to need to go there to buy pillows and toothbrushes and underwear.

Cigarettes and alcohol are extremely expensive no matter where you shop. Cigarettes start at $13 per pack. $16 for Marlboros. Six packs of beer start at $11. $16 for Heineken. So if you've got chemical additions you're either going to have to give them up or give up every other luxury in your life.

Gas (aka petrol) is about $2.09 per liter. That's $7.91 per gallon. You may consider getting a bicycle (aka push-bike). I have to warn you though, the only thing Kiwis hate more than bicyclists on the road are bicyclists on the sidewalk (aka footpath).

Luckily there are plenty of free activities you can do to have fun in New Zealand. There are more beaches and hiking trails than one person can visit in their life. There's always a cultural festival going on somewhere. There are plenty of art museums. Auckland literally has over 800 parks. If you want to socialize you can find plenty of meetup groups online where you can connect with other world travelers. New Zealand tries really hard to make itself accessible to visitors. So almost every town in New Zealand that's worth going to has a tourist information office somewhere near the center of town. Just head there, and you'll find out everything you need to know about the local area.

The Department of Conservation has a lot of free camp sites, but they're so far off the beaten track you'll need a GPS to find them. And of course, the beach is always free.

10 THINGS AMERICANS WILL GET USED TO

AFTER LIVING IN NEW ZEALAND FOR SIX MONTHS

1. Driving on the left-hand side of the road for the first time is more terrifying than you'd think, but you'll get used to it within a week. That or you'll die in a fiery, head-on collision. Eventually, you'll stop having anxiety attacks every time you drive through a roundabout.

2. Your co-workers wearing the same shirt as you: That's because there is one mall. And in that mall are two stores that you buy clothes from. These are the same two stores for all twenty-something women that you work with.

3. Snubbing your nose at grocery store veggies: You get them fresh from the farm of course. Plus, in the winter the vegetable selection at normal grocery stores get real sad and real expensive.

4. Your new diet: Nobody tells you this, but when you move to a new country you have to adapt your diet to what food is available locally. When you change what goes in your body you change what comes out of your body.

5. Chemical withdrawals: Cigarettes cost $13-$19 per pack. Beer costs $11-$19 per six pack, and liquor is something you only buy on very special occasions. Since you just spent all your money moving to a foreign country you can't afford to be an addict.

6. Going to bed at 9: Because everything is closed by 7, and two hours of staring at you partner is enough for anyone.

7. A diminishing dislike for cops: You can go weeks without seeing a cop, and when you do see them you don't have to be

afraid of them, because unlike the cops in the United States, their motto isn't, "To terrorize and fleece."

8. Seeing people not wearing shoes. They're everywhere, and that's fine.

9. Real ethnic restaurants owned and operated by real ethnic families with a real ethnic atmosphere.

10. Calling NZ home: it may have taken six months but now remember your phone number and address.

And one more for fun: You'll finally accept that you'll never be able to pronounce local words with your American accent. There might have been hope if you were only up against a local language, but in NZ it's the British version of the local language. Look away and mumble.

HOW TO SPEAK KIWI

• "sweet as." – This is like saying, "Cool." Also, you can substitute "sweet" with any adjective.

 "Living in New Zealand is sweet as, bro." or "That shirt is expensive as."

• "tog" – a bathing suite

"Grab your togs. We're going to Hot Water Beach in Coromandel this weekend."

• "getting pissed" or "getting on the piss" – getting drunk

"My mates and I were getting on the piss a bit at the pub last night."

• "taking the piss" – mocking or harassing someone. It can also be used to describe "pulling someone's leg."

"One of my mates got bashed at the pub last night for taking the piss at this hori fellow." Or "My friend told me he slept with a sweet as girl from the pub last night, and I told to stop taking the piss out of me."

• "hori" – an adjective to describe someone who is trashy, unkempt, low class and uncultured. It's the New Zealand equivalent of calling someone trailer trash. It used to be a derogatory term specifically directed at Maori, but anyone can be a hori now.

"My mates and I were getting on the piss at the pub last night and we were taking the piss out of this hori fellow because he was wearing togs and smelled like sheep."

- "pie" – a meat pie

"For lunch I got a pie at the dairy."

- "dairy" – a convenience store

"I'm going to run down to the dairy to pick up a pie and cigarettes."

- "tea" – lunch

"Want to join me for tea? I'm going to McDonalds."

- "full stop" – a period (the grammatical kind)

"You need to put a full stop at the end of that sentence or it will be a run-on sentence."

This next word isn't different from English, but if you want to sound Kiwi, try to use it at least twice in every conversation:

- "heaps" – a lot

"Don't take heaps of luggage when you travel. It's heaps more trouble than it's worth."

- "capsicum" – bell peppers

"Would you like capsicum on your salad?"

- "smoko" – a smoke break

"I can't talk now, but my smoko is in 15 minutes."

- "fanny" – A women's private parts.

"Does this dress make my fanny look big?" "No. It doesn't make your vagina look big."

- "torch" – Flashlight

"Make sure to bring your torch on the night hike."

- "suss" – To finish or complete a task

"Have you sussed your homework yet?" "Yeah, bro. I got that sussed hours ago."

- "jelly" – Jello, not jam.

"Would you like a peanut butter and jelly sandwich?" "That's nasty, bro. Why would I put jello on a sandwich?"

- "jandal" – a sandal or flip flop

"Don't forget to wear your jandals to the beach. The sand is hot enough to burn your feet."

- "lollie" – candy

"Mommy, can we get some lollies when we go through the checkout stand at the grocery store?" "No, they'll rot your teeth."

ODE TO THE NEW ZEALAND WINTER

When we first started researching moving to New Zealand almost two years ago we kept coming across the topic of how cold it is in the winter. At first, I just brushed it off as spoiled Americans whining. I was wrong. It's a big enough of a deal to warrant an essay on. As you're reading this, if you get the impression I'm boringly commenting on some arbitrary issue, I can assure you that learning about the heat in Texas during the summer before going there is as important as learning about the cold in New Zealand during the winter before going there.

Keep in mind though that I've been in Auckland the whole time I've been here and can only speak for Auckland weather. The winter here is as rainy as any tropical island. It rains almost every day during the winter; the rain starts and stops abruptly; a heavy, torrential downpour will hit your side of town and be cleared up in 1 hour while someone you're on the phone with across town won't see a drop of rain.; sometimes it's just permanently misty for days at a time; every once a while you might get a few dry days in a row, but it's usually rainy for so long that you barely even notice the rain anymore and you don't rush in a panicked frenzy out of the rain when it comes.

The winter temperature stays between 40 and 50 degrees Fahrenheit (give or take 10 degrees) all winter long. We never have to scrape frost off our windshield in the morning, but we can never go a day without a jacket either.

So the winter isn't painfully, lethally cold like in Canada. The temperature doesn't yo-yo between 10 degrees and 85 degrees like in Texas either. It's just a dull, wet cold for 6+ months straight. Often the weather will warm up around lunch time and be perfectly wonderful, but you'll probably be at work during those hours. The mornings, evenings and nights when you're out and about will be soggy and sad.

This is bad news for people with allergies to mold. Mold is a real issue that you're going to have to deal with eventually if you live here. Be prepared to spend $150 on a dehumidifier.

The point is it's permanently uncomfortably cold here during the winter. This wouldn't be a problem worth mentioning, but insulation and central heating and air-conditioning haven't hit it big here like they have in Texas.

In Texas,, a fireplace is a more of a novelty than a necessity. You might light it on Christmas or "cuddle night" but that's about it. And you take off your jacket when you come inside. In New Zealand there's always the smell of someone's toasty fire coming from a chimney somewhere near you. When you come inside you take off your outside jacket and put on your inside jacket, robe, hoodie or sweater. Some people (like Amber) get dressed under the covers in the morning, and everybody has an electric blanket.

When you go to work, there's a decent chance there won't be much difference. Amber works at a school that uses space heaters to heat large classrooms. She teaches while wearing her coat, mittens and a bear hat. I work the night shift in a warehouse. I wear pajama pants under my pants, a thermal shirt, an over shirt, a zip-up sweater thing, a polyester vest, a sports jacket, fingerless gloves and a beanie to work every day...I mean, night. I wake up in the cold. I'm cold during my free time at home. I work in the cold, and when I get home from a hard, cold night of work, I come home to the cold. Then I go to sleep in the cold and wake up again in the cold. The dull, wet cold is a constant companion.

Why don't they insulate their houses you ask? Well, I suspect it's because it's so expensive to ship anything here that they never really got the resources to insulate most homes or install central heating and air-conditioning. So the locals have been living with the dull, wet cold for generations. So they don't whine about it as much as Americans. In fact, Kiwis don't believe in the cold. They're convinced they live in Hawaii. So you'll see them walking around barefoot wearing Stubbies in the dead of winter while you're bundled up in a snowsuit.

On the upside, because of the constant winter rain and mild summers, it's always luscious and green here. If Ireland hadn't taken the title "The Emerald Isle" first, New Zealand probably would have gotten it. New Zealand is so fertile that plants grow in the trees. Seriously.

BUSINESS CULTURE IN NEW ZEALAND

New Zealand's business culture's greatest advantage is also its greatest weakness: lower standards of professionalism. People walk around offices without their shoes on. They drink alcohol during business hours sometimes. They cuss with the customers. They dress a little more casual, and upper management doesn't talk to lower ranking workers like second class citizens quite as disgracefully as is standard business practice in corporate America. The work environment is a little more laid back in New Zealand, and you can have a little more fun.

However, New Zealand business practices often lack structure, efficiency and reliability. The business mindset is relatively amateur here. I suspect that's partly because there's so little competition in any given industry that there's little incentive to tighten standards. I see a bit of tribal thinking used in business decision-making processes too. Businesses will treat other businesses poorly or favorably based on personal attitudes, and businesses will stab other businesses in the back if it benefits them. Obviously, these generalizations aren't universal, but there is a bit of a Wild West approach to business here.

Plus, wages are fairly low. That's why a lot of immigrants will come to New Zealand until they get their citizenship and then move to Australia as soon as possible. You'll make more money in Australia and have more options. Plus, the weather is generally nicer. That's just a fact of life that drains New Zealand of quality workers and is a wound to Kiwi's pride.

There's a silver lining to all these negatives though. New Zealand is an entrepreneur's paradise. There are a lot of good ideas that aren't being implemented because Kiwis aren't aggressive in business and don't think outside the box. Plus, since the economy is so small and so far outside standard international shipping routes, if you can fill a shipping container full of just about anything and get it to New Zealand you can sell it at a premium price.

While you may not have been an outside-the-box thinker back in your home country, simply going to New Zealand where everyone else thinks differently and is stuck in their old ways automatically makes you a novel thinker and gives you an advantage. No matter what business you start up you've got a pretty solid chance of success simply because there's more demand for most industries than there is competition. If nothing else, if you want to sell luxury goods such as art, jewelry, T-shirts and knick-knacks, there's a thriving tourism industry that rotates new, frivolous customers through the country every month.

THE NEW ZEALAND SHEEP FENCE NETWORK

If you live in New Zealand long enough you're eventually going to go hiking. Probably sooner rather than later. There are hiking trails everywhere, even where there doesn't need to be hiking trails. In a small town near Tauranga there's a hiking trail that weaves through its downtown strip in addition to the existing sidewalk... because it would be too boring to just walk on the sidewalk that's already there.

Finding out that there's a breathtaking hiking trail right around the corner or stumbling on a city with a superfluous hiking trail woven through the downtown strip are little just two examples of idiosyncratic things that make you smile in New Zealand. Another example is that it's completely normal for these hiking trails to cut across private property where sheep graze.

It's super cool that you can just walk on and off people's property. In America, the sheep would be a health and safety hazard. The entrance would have to be wheelchair accessible, and there'd have to be a water fountain and toilets available. There'd be signs warning you not to shove rocks or sticks in your eyes, and it'd cost $10 per person. In New Zealand, if you want to go walk over there... then you can just go walk over there.

It's not that New Zealand doesn't have fences demarcating where private and public property meet. When a hiking trail meets private property there will be a (usually) very basic, wooden step that you can use to hop over the fence.

Now that you understand that New Zealand is covered in a patchwork of countryside woven together by age-old, public walkways then you can understand a social phenomenon that exists in New Zealand that I call "The Sheep Fence Network."

Kiwis may or may not have their own word for this phenomenon, but it's a significant enough facet of Kiwi culture for someone to coin a term for it.

It stems from the fact that New Zealand is a pretty small place where everybody knows everybody, and it's extremely common for people to move to different cities. Despite how much Kiwis migrate within their own country they still really, really, really value family, heritage and history. So they don't just fly the nest and never write home as is often the case in America. They take their social connections with them.

If any one Kiwi doesn't know another Kiwi specifically, he will still know 15 people who know that person. It's like 6 Degrees to Kevin Bacon except with a lot fewer degrees. If you're ever at a bar with your Kiwi bloke friends, and another Kiwi enters the conversation and nobody knows that person, you'll probably have to sit through 23 minutes of oral history while everyone figures out how many people they know who knows someone who knows the other person. So everyone knows everyone indirectly through this informal sheep fence social network.

Unfortunately for immigrants, Kiwis will often have an inside connection on jobs. This isn't sinister; if one of your friends asked you for a job you'd probably going to give it to them. You might even give your brother's friend, or your best friend's friend preference before you even advertise a job to people with hard-to-understand accents who don't get all your inside jokes.

You can use this to your advantage though. If you know you're going to move to New Zealand then get on the Internet and try to impress a few people in New Zealand. Make some professional pen pals and then drop their names every chance possible. I didn't actually do that myself, and I've never known anyone who has, but it seems like it would work really well in theory.

And don't worry about it too much anyway. There are 10 million reasons why this may never be a problem for you, but once you've lived in New Zealand long enough to establish your own catalog of references you'll be able to play the name game with blokes at the bar and enjoy all the perks of being accepted into the sheep fence network.

HEALTHCARE IN NEW ZEALAND

I've been planning on writing a post on healthcare in New Zealand for some time, but I don't have that much experience with it. So I've been putting it off. It's an important topic though, and people want to know about it. So I've decided to go ahead and share my observations and thoughts on it. Just understand that what I'm about to write isn't a definitive account of New Zealand's healthcare written by an expert in the field.

I want to kick this off by talking about healthcare in America. If you apply for a temporary work visa you have to get a physical performed that basically says you have all your limbs and you don't have aids. If you apply for a permanent residence visa you have to get a pretty thorough medical screening done. Amber and I had to go through this back in Texas before we moved here. Amber had health insurance through the school she worked for, but I was doing contract I.T. work and didn't have any health insurance. Amber ended up paying about $500 for her tests. I couldn't find a doctor who would even see me without health insurance. Probably someone would have, but I couldn't find them. Luckily Amber's mother (who lived in Chicago) had just got engaged to a man who had a brother in San Antonio who was a doctor, and he agreed to do my physical for free. However, his clinic didn't do the blood and urine tests. So I had to go somewhere else that charged me $300. I failed my lipids test because I'd eaten a pizone from Pizza Hut 6 hours before the test. You're supposed to fast for 8 hours. So I had to shell out another $150 to redo half my blood work. So I ended up paying almost as much as Amber just for the lab work, and that was only because I was lucky enough to be able to get the actual doctor visit done pro bono. Even though Amber got all her work done for about $500, there's no telling how much she paid in monthly insurance fees overall.

They have a saying in America (that they don't have anywhere else) that "business is war," and healthcare is big business. This means there's a war on patients in America. I was just Skyping a friend back in Texas a few days ago, and he had his finger ripped open by a dog and had to have stitches, but he had to wait in the emergency room waiting room for six hours before he could see a doctor. He's unemployed, but his wife was in the military. So the military paid for it. If he didn't get to take advantage of the military's socialized medical care I don't know what he would have done...or if the doctors would have seen him at all. As exclusive and expensive as healthcare in America is you do get what you pay for...some of the time.

Point in fact, I'm a twin, and typical for twins, I was born prematurely. My twin was fine, but my heart hadn't finished developing, and the patent ductus arteriosus in my heart wasn't done developing. So I was born a "blue baby." A valve in my heart wasn't working, and oxygen-rich blood wasn't circulating through my body. So I had to be air-lifted to Houston where they had one of the best heart surgery hospitals in the world. If I'd been born at home by a midwife or been born in New Zealand I might not have survived. However, my father was a chemical engineer at the time. So my family was in a prime position to save my life. They paid an arm and a leg for it, but I'm here today. If my dad wasn't a chemical engineer then I probably wouldn't have fared so well. Also, that was over 30 years ago, and a lot has changed since then.

Michael Moore probably wouldn't have made "Sicko" back then. I'm no fan of Michael Moore, but that movie raises valid points.

The medical industry in America today is designed to get patients out "quicker and sicker" (do a Google search for that term) to maximize profits. In America, if you can't pay extortionate prices for your medical care you just don't get it. If you can pay your premiums you still get the bare minimum treatment. However, if you have as much money as "Magic" Johnson then you can literally survive AIDS. That's America. The rich get the best, and the poor get nothing.

Now let's fast-forward to after Amber and I immigrated to New Zealand. Remember how much we paid for our immigration physicals? Well, walking around downtown Auckland we saw signs advertising immigration physicals for $250. New Zealand doesn't have completely "free" socialized medical care like the United States Military, but it has subsidized medical care. So instead of giving all your money to the insurance companies so the CEO can buy a new yacht, you give a little bit of your money to the government so your neighbor can see a doctor.

I first felt the benefit from this when I tried to give up smoking last year. In America, I paid $40 for a pack of nicotine patches. In New Zealand, I got 3 months' worth for free.

I have some pretty nasty warts on the bottom of my foot that I just left alone while I was in America because I couldn't afford to have anything done about them. I saw a doctor in New Zealand for $17. That price is pretty standard. Some places charge like $40 for a doctor's visit, and Kiwis get red in the face about how expensive that is. Anyway, my consultation was $17 because I went to a shady doctor's office on the poor side of town. Their trash can was literally a shopping bag hanging off the oxygen tank. They agreed to cut the warts off for $150. There was hair all over the pillow on the operating table, but I didn't care enough to complain because I was just so happy to be getting medical attention at all. After the operation, I took my prescription next door to the pharmacist and got a bag full of painkillers and antibiotics. The cost for each of the bottles was $3. It was just a flat rate of $3 for everything where in America I would have been lucky to pay $3 per pill.

Granted, the doctor's office I went to was practically a bodega, and the warts grew back anyway. I went back for a checkup and told the doctor it looked like the warts were growing back, and they assured me that what I was seeing was just scar tissue. Since then I changed my doctor office and saw a new doctor at a more professional looking clinic about the warts. This new doctor charged me $17 for the visit and told me that verruca warts on the bottom of your feet are almost impossible to get rid of by surgery and that they would go away eventually on their own. So I left with my warts still there and with the reassurance that the doctor wasn't trying to rip me off.

That's as much personal experience as I've had with medicine in New Zealand. Granted, I didn't go to the nicest clinic in Auckland, and I'm sure the first place I went will be shut down by health inspectors eventually. However, I wouldn't have had that experience at all in America if for no other reason then I wouldn't have been able to see a doctor in America.

It comes down to this, if having the absolute best health-care in the world is your top priority and money is no object then you might consider staying in America (close to a major city like Houston). However, if affordable, regular healthcare is more important to you then you'll fare better in New Zealand. Even then, if you can afford to pay American prices then you could afford to fly back to America for the occasional major surgery.

That's not to say though that New Zealand doesn't have hospitals that are fully capable performing major life-saving operations.

New Zealand also requires employees to pay into a program called ACC, which takes very good care of you if you get injured at work. Personally, I absolutely love living in New Zealand knowing that I can afford to see a doctor whenever I need to and will be able to get prescriptions filled without going bankrupt. I'm more than happy to see a New Zealand doctor, and I'll even bet my life on that. Having said that, I'm glad I was born in America...30 years ago.

I hope that helps.

RELIGION IN NEW ZEALAND

In order to understand the role religion plays in modern New Zealand culture, it helps to understand the role religion plays in cultures in general. Anytime you analyze religions that have diffused into foreign cultures you'll see the new religion wipe out some of the old cultural folkways and norms. For example, ascetic religions (like Christianity) tend to turn wild, promiscuous pagan cultures more Puritanical. However, cultures will also wipe out parts of invasive religions that are too incompatible with the beliefs/practices the locals' ancestors handed down to them. For example, most Christians today believe slavery is ethically wrong even though the Bible approves and even promotes the practice of slavery multiple times.

So invasive religions end up getting changed by their host cultures as much as they change it. The perfect example is how some African American Christians have pictures hanging in their living rooms of a strong Negro-skinned Jesus while next door their Caucasian Christian neighbors have a picture of a blonde haired, blue-eyed suburban Jesus even though Jesus (if he existed) would have looked Middle Eastern.

Christianity has definitely left its mark on New Zealand culture. Christianity's arbitrary Puritanical moral code has rooted itself in New Zealand civil law...and yet those laws are different than Christian-based laws in other Christian countries. For example, in New Zealand the age you can legally drink and have sex are lower than in other Christian nations. Yet, New Zealand Christians still won't let gays marry.

Christian Kiwi politicians might have woven puritanical Christian asceticism deeper into the law books, except the majority of

New Zealand's citizens aren't western-thinking Christians. Immigrants from Asia and the Pacific islands make up a significant percentage of New Zealand's population and thus New Zealand's cultural identity. Plus, Christians from different cultures have brought their own distinct flavors of Christianity with them that clash with other cultures' expression of Christianity fracturing the greater Christian culture in New Zealand instead of giving it strength in numbers.

Think of New Zealand as a petri dish. Every time a new demographic appeared in New Zealand new bacteria got dropped into the dish. Originally there was only a glob of brown Maori bacteria. Then a huge glob of white Pakeha bacteria got dropped into the dish, and it spread and turned the Maori bacteria a few shades whiter, but the Maori bacteria also turned the white pakeha bacteria a little bit brown. Then a small but steady stream of yellow and red bacteria started dropping into the dish from India and Asia. While those four cultures were trying to diffuse to the point of equilibrium tiny drops of bacteria of other cultures from all over the world have been splattering into the dish as well. As a result, no single cultural or religious identity has been able to claim New Zealand. Since solidarity isn't possible Kiwi culture has adapted by keeping their religion to themselves for the most part.

It shouldn't be surprising that Kiwis would settle on such a lasses faire solution to the question of religious identity since island culture is laid back, and British colonial culture is private and tactful. When all of those cultural tendencies are combined they produce people who don't fight with their neighbors over religious differences.

HOW TO USE THE MGI BILL OVERSEAS

The Montgomery GI Bill (AKA MGI Bill) is a scholarship/grant given by the United States Department of Veteran Affairs to veterans of the United States Military. If you're not an honorably discharged veteran of the United States military then this information isn't going to be useful to you.

Here's what you need to know if you're planning on using the MGI Bill at a foreign school:

You can only use the MGI Bill at accredited higher education institutions that have been approved by the MGI Bill. Most major universities in the world have already been approved. I used to have a link that showed all the approved foreign schools, but that link is dead now, and I can't find one that works. So you'll need to contact the VA and ask for the link/list if you can't find it online. Note that it takes them 1-3 weeks to respond to E-mails (if ever). It's quicker just to call them, but be prepared to wait on hold for a long time.

Every school that's approved by the VA has someone who is already authorized/designated as the point of contact between that school and the VA. Chances are it will be someone in the foreign student office. That person doesn't work for the VA. They're just a person who is designated as the school's liaison with the VA, and they may not be very familiar with how the MGI Bill works, but they can get all their answers by contacting the VA themselves. So when you find out who your school's VA rep is, make sure you give them all the contact information for the VA that exists. You won't actually file any paperwork with the VA yourself. It's the liaison's responsibility to do all that stuff. So you don't have to worry about that. You just have to worry about keeping your liaison on task.

The VA can tell you who the VA rep at your foreign school is. Find that out before you arrive on campus so you can go to the student services office and ask to see that person by name. Or, once you have that person's name, you can find their E-mail address from the school's website and start E-mailing him/her before you even show up in-country. But if you just show up at the student services desk at your foreign school one day and ask to see "the VA rep who handles the MGI Bill" they're not going to have any idea what you're talking about, and you're going to spend a very frustrating day running around trying to find that person.

Not only does your school have to be approved, but so does your degree program. If it's not already approved then your MGIBill liaison at the foreign school will have to submit an application to have it approved. Unless a US veteran has already used the MGI Bill for your degree program at your school then you'll have to get your liaison to request that it be approved. As long as you're going to an accredited school this isn't a big deal. The liaison just needs to turn in the paperwork, and in a few weeks the program will be approved. Nobody really scrutinizes the program with a fine tooth comb. After all, the program is already an accredited program at an accredited school. The VA just has to process the paperwork as a formality. But it's important to make sure this is done well before you start your classes or you may not get your first semester funded.

To get your BAH (personal living expenses money), the VA will either mail a check to your foreign address (which can take weeks) or they'll direct deposit it into an American bank account. They won't direct deposit it into a foreign account. I had to have my BAH deposited into my American account and take the cash out from an ATM when I needed it. So make sure you still have an American bank account and an active ATM card.

The VA pays your tuition directly to the school. So you don't have to worry about that, but they send the school a check, which takes weeks to arrive, and the exchange rate will change during that time. Plus, you'll likely be charged an exorbitant exchange rate. Between those two factors, the check might not cover the cost of your tuition. If that's the case, you just eat the cost yourself. On the other hand, if the exchange rate swings in your favor you could get to keep some extra money, but don't hold your breath on that ever happening.

OUR NINE MONTH RETROSPECTIVE

At the time of writing this, we've lived in New Zealand for 9 months. We've both got fulltime jobs, and I've been at my job long enough to get a promotion. We've gotten used to driving on the left-hand side of the road, and we can get around town without a map. The other side of town isn't a scary mystery anymore. We've made a few friends and aren't completely alone anymore. Basically, New Zealand doesn't feel like a foreign country anymore. And actually, we probably reached that point about 2 months ago. So if you're wondering how long it takes to get through the initial, stressful, scary, foreign, lonely, make or break phase of moving to a foreign country, I'd put it at about 6-7 months...9 months tops. But obviously, that's going to be different for everyone. If you already have a business or social connections here or have visited New Zealand before you could probably shorten that time frame.

Realizing we've passed this milestone I thought it was time to do a little retrospective on our move. Did it accomplish what we were hoping? What surprised us? Would we do anything differently if we could do it all over again? What did we do right?

To the first question I would have to say, without reservation, that yes, the move accomplished its purpose. We are enjoying a significantly higher quality of life in New Zealand than we were in Texas, and that has nothing to do with our attitude, optimism or any other mode of perception you can learn from any positive thinking self-help book. New Zealand is just decades ahead of America in terms of the benefits it provides its citizens and in eliminating the ills of society. Nature also gave New Zealand an unfair advantage by putting so much fun stuff to do here. Granted, New Zealand does have its own shortcomings just like anywhere else, but our burdens here are light and are far outweighed by the benefits.

What surprised us? Well, the housing took a while to figure out. In Auckland at least, housing is very expensive. So unless you have a very high paying job you're going to have to live with flatmates. It's very, very, very common for full grown adults and even elderly people to live with other grown adult and elderly flatmates. And I don't mean you'll be living like that during a transitional phase of your life. I mean that's just life. And the best way to find a flat is to go to www.trademe.co.nz. I wish I'd known that before we moved here.

If I could do anything differently I would have brought more money, and I would have sold my house back in Austin. We came here with about $14,000 US. Most of that was sent right back to America to pay our property manager for unexpected repairs to what used to be our home and is now our rental property...or maybe he's just been ripping us off by charging us for superfluous repairs. Since we're in New Zealand we have no way to know or to do anything about it.

Trying to deal with a property halfway across the world has been a monumental headache, and every penny we've sent back has been one less penny we had to spend on establishing our new life. As a result, we had to stretch our money and count our pennies the first few months we were here.

I was really surprised how stressful the whole experience was. I've lived in 3 different countries for a total of 7 years when I was in the US military. So I figured this trip would be easy for a seasoned world traveler such as myself. What I didn't take into account was that in the military I had a job and a house waiting for me, and it was impossible to fail. Hell, you literally got a checklist when you got off the plane that told you everything you needed to do. Moving to a foreign country on my own I, or rather "we," had to figure out everything on our own and fight for our survival at a game that has no guarantees and a high rate of failure.

If I could do the trip over again I would have brought a calendar with me and premarked events for every week for the first 6 months. Once a week I would mark a day to force ourselves to get out of the house and experience something new. Once a week I would mark a day to talk to my significant other about our frustrations with each other. I would have set concrete goals for job hunting. I would have premarked festivals that I knew were coming up. I would have also marked the deadlines for various immigration paperwork. All of this would have helped cope with stress, overcome the hurdles of moving to another country and provided structure, predictability and purpose to our lives after having hit the reset button.

Another thing I would have done differently is set up an account at www.skype.com before I left. Getting to see and talk to our family and friends back home for free whenever we want has been a huge source of comfort. I knew about Skype, but I thought it was really complicated to set up. Turns out it's easier than making a Facebook account.

What did we do right? First of all, we took a chance. There's no telling how many people dream of starting a better life but are too afraid to let go of what little they have and decide to live out the rest of their short, irreplaceable lives in cold comfort instead. Ironically, in a lot of ways, that's actually the sane, responsible thing to do. Moving to a new country is a gamble, and gambling isn't responsible. But we stacked the bet in our favor with determination, flexibility and creativity, and we won. If we'd listened to reason and stayed where we were and kept our demeaning jobs and kept fighting traffic every day we would have lost.

Another thing we did right was starting our residency visa a year before moving here. We didn't know you could apply for a working holiday visa and a residency visa at the same time. So we didn't apply for our working holiday visa until after we got here. That was a big mistake, because you can't finalize your residency visa until you get a job. Nobody will hire you if you don't can't legally work. So it took us a month to figure that out after we got here and another 2 months to get the working holiday visa. Plus, we had to spend money on that we hadn't budgeted. But it would have been much worse if we hadn't started the residency visa paperwork a year in advance. So that was good.

Once we arrived in country we were smart to book a hostel in advance for the first few weeks. That gave us a cheap (though regrettably uncomfortable) place to start from that we weren't locked into. It was also a good idea to get a hostel downtown so we could really jump into the Auckland experience. Once we left the hostel we made another good decision in finding a series of places with short term leases so we could hop around until we both found jobs and could live close to both of them and live with cool people. It was stressful constantly moving, but living in an inconvenient place with anal-retentive, passive aggressive flatmates was much more stressful. By staying flexible and mobile we managed to end up in a quaint house right on the beach with some pretty cool people.

The last smart thing we did was adopting Tiko. Nothing says normality like having a pet. Plus, it gives you something to care about and be cared by. Plus, Tiko is just awesome. I've never had a cat that will sleep under the covers and sit on my shoulder while I cook.

OUR THREE YEAR RETROSPECTIVE

So we've been living in New Zealand for 3 years now. It took about 9 months to get used to living here and two years to say everything we have to say about the immigration process. We've only written a couple of blogs in the past year because we've run out of things to say about the immigration process/experience. Even now as I try to think of things to say all I can think of is to re-emphasize things we've already said.

The first thing I have to say is that neither of us have any regrets moving to New Zealand. If we had to do it all over again we would have left America sooner. Kiwis are friendlier than Americans, and this isn't just a statistic from a survey. When you live in New Zealand you are constantly impressed by how friendly people are. Granted, there are some horrible people, but the overall culture is refreshingly friendly.

Not only are people friendly, but they're also generally accepting of other races and cultures. New Zealand only has a fraction of the racism, religious bigotry, gang violence and homophobia as America. There are only a few places in New Zealand where you should be afraid to go outside at night, and you're never going to have to worry about getting car jacked. Even hitchhiking is so safe it's still a national past time.

One of the best things about New Zealand is how absolutely, ridiculously beautiful it is. It's so fantastically beautiful that people come from all over the world to film fantasy movies here. You'd have to go to Norway or the Alps to see scenery as beautiful as New Zealand's.

Having said that, New Zealand isn't without its problems. It's got its own idiosyncratic issues that are easy to ignore, but it has at least four big problems that are a constant thorn in my side. The biggest one is the oppressive economy. Wages are low, and the cost of living is high. You feel the financial squeeze immediately when you move to New Zealand, and it never goes away.

The second biggest problem is the inadequate insulation in the houses. Every winter you live with the never ending cold. Seriously, I lived in Germany for 2 years, and even though the temperature in Germany was much colder than New Zealand, this country feels colder because you can't escape it... unless you're rich. The summers are next to perfect in New Zealand, but the winters can be... daunting.

The third problem is the lack of professionalism in New Zealand business culture. You get jerked around and charged nonsensical prices. Also, bosses aren't constrained by modern, first world standards of professionalism either. There are probably some phenomenal bosses somewhere in New Zealand, but all the ones I've met fly by the cuff and manage their employees irrationally. There are good things to be said about New Zealand's lax standards of professionalism though. For instance, I'm typing this at work while drinking a beer, and I wear shoes to work maybe once a week. So that's good. I can thank New Zealand's low standards of professionalism for that, but the downside is that trying to get quality work/services from Kiwi businesses can be... daunting.

The last problem with New Zealand is the high population of South Pacific red necks who have never left the region they were born in and have no interest in being a part of the outside world.... or being intelligent in general. This problem is offset by the huge international community in New Zealand. This year my best mates were British, German, Estonian, French and Finnish. I've lived with flatmates from all over the globe, and that's awesome, but there's still a huge percentage of people in this country who just aren't switched on and never will be. Granted, every country has these people. I just wish New Zealand had less.

These are just my personal views. Different people love and hate different things about New Zealand. So take this for what it's worth.

HOME FOR THE HOLIDAYS: AN EXPAT LOOKS AT LONELINESS

This past Christmas Amber and I didn't fly home to visit friends and family back in America, and none of our friends or family from America flew out to visit us. Instead, we all just celebrated the holidays on our own and put the photos on Facebook for anyone who cared to see later.

Some people couldn't imagine spending a holiday like that. I knew people in the military who lived overseas and would fly back to America every Christmas regardless of the unfair ticket prices, the hassle of holiday travel or the fact that they would burn four days of leave in transit. They didn't factor those problems into deciding whether or not the trip would be worth it because it was a given that they would go home for the holidays. The idea of not going never occurred to them.

At the time I saw those people as weak. The only reason some of them were stationed overseas was because the military forced them to deploy there. Even after they were forced out of their comfort zone they were still too codependent on their traditional support structures to leave the nest completely and experience the amazing opportunities life had presented them with. So they went home every chance they got and whined about it whenever they couldn't.

There was some validity to my vain perspective, but there was a downside to my sense of geographical liberation. Case in point, I spent my last Christmas in Germany with 4 other guys about the same age as me. We bought a keg, put it in the snow on the balcony and spent Christmas Night drinking and playing video games until we blacked out. As awesome as that was I suspect we were all a little bummed we didn't have a warm, clean, well-lighted place to spend the holidays where everybody knows your name; the closest thing we had to that feeling we found in bars.

If you're going to leave your foreign country only to end up spending your holidays drinking and reminiscing about where you came from then you'd probably be better off staying where you're at. If you do spend your expat holidays whining then that's ultimately your fault, because holidays can be a great opportunity to make the most of your expat experience...as I've come to learn.

The first Christmas Amber and I spent in New Zealand we celebrated with a large Fijian family. It was cultural, educational and inebriating. Our first Thanksgiving in New Zealand (which they don't celebrate here) we found an American expat meetup group on the internet that was throwing a huge, free dinner and social mixer event. So we went and met a lot of Libertarians...which surprised me, and I still can't explain.

This past Christmas Amber and I took a month and a half long road trip down to the bottom of New Zealand and back up to Auckland. Amber worked with a teacher whose parents lived on the South Island. So we all met up there for Christmas. The family we stayed with took us in, gave us a tour of the local area and showed us a good time all around.

One night we were all sitting around the dining room table drinking wine or scotch or beer, and the mother leaned over the table and asked Amber and I with a meaningful tone of voice, "So where do you call home?" with extra emphasis on the word, "home."

The thing about that is, I've never lived in the same town for more than three consecutive years...in my entire life. Amber bounced around quite a bit as well. We met in Hawaii, thousands of miles from where either of us were raised. It's not that we were orphans. We have families, and it's not that we hate everyone in our families. Amber and I have a few tight bonds with a few family members, but there's too much bad blood on all the branches in general for either of our families to be able to have big family reunions without somebody stabbing someone with BBQ utensil.

Since we hadn't been raised with deep roots it was no more out of character for us to be spending our holidays in a foreign country with strangers than it was for Amber's coworker to be spending her holiday with her family in her hometown. I explained to our dinner hosts in a few words why Amber and I don't have a place in America that we call "home." Then they asked the next logical question, "So do you consider New Zealand your home now?" The thing about that is, a place becomes your home slowly over time. Personally, for me, I've moved so many times and had so many two-year-friends in the military that I don't get attached to places or even people very quickly anymore. I love it in New Zealand just like I loved a lot of places I've lived, but after two years I still don't feel completely rooted, though I'm sure some people would.

In time I'll come to feel like New Zealand is my home, and I'll come to value friendships I've made here as important as family, and I'm looking forward to it because it's going to be awesome, but there's another long-term down-side to the great adventure I'm taking that would-be expats should be aware of.

My nieces are growing up in photographs. Every time I talk to my brothers I have less and less in common with them to talk about. Every year it becomes more and more the case that the only thing I have in common with my original friends and family is the past.

That's just how long distance relationships go. You don't want to admit it to yourself, much less them, and for a while, you pretend like it isn't happening. You keep in touch on Skype and by E-mail. Maybe you even write a blog to help maintain a connection, but at the end of the day, you may as well be living on different planets. And on each planet life goes on. If you're the type to spend Christmas drinking alone listening to emo music the thought might occur to you that as far as your old life is concerned you might as well be dead, and without being dramatic, there's a little truth to that. Your old family and friends are getting on with their lives without you just as surely as you'll get on with your life any time one of your relatives dies.

But that doesn't mean expatriating has to be a form of suicide nor does it mean you're abandoning anyone. Life is meant to be lived. Nests are meant to be left. How much does it honor the people who raised you if you spend your life hiding from life's challenges and never step out of your comfort zone? If you want to play devil's advocate you could ask how much you owe it to the people who care about you to maintain an active role their lives. We could argue all day about that, and if you become an expat you'll probably end up arguing with yourself about it eventually.

In the end, this is an issue every expat has to work out on their own. If you think you might have trouble bringing closure to that issue then you might consider finding a therapist to talk after you immigrate. That doesn't make you weak. That makes you resourceful. I'd probably do it myself if I could afford to. Short of that, I recommend lots of introspection and socialization to keep away the existential blues. And remember that expatriating is like anything else in life; it's what you make of it.

FIVE WAYS TRAVELING MAKES YOU A BETTER PERSON

I've visited about 19 different countries, and I've lived (with a job and mailing address) in 5. I've had some crazy adventures, and I could tell you some crazy stories that are more amusing than most of the sitcoms you're going to watch this month, but I'm not going to tell you about them because I've learned that nobody wants to hear about how you're better than them. I'm not saying I'm better than anyone else; what I mean is that if you tell people stories that make them jealous then they tend to resent you for it because it inherently comes off as bragging no matter how innocent your intentions are. So people don't want to hear it; they want you to hear their stories. Dale Carnegie explained this concept in his famous treatise on human nature "How To Win Friends and Influence People." If you want to make friends, you let them talk, and you act like you're jealous of them.

So I do my best to refrain from telling anyone (even world travelers) too much about my world travels, and even then I only talk about stories that are pertinent to the topic of conversation at hand. While this tactic keeps me from alienating people, there's something valuable lost by it. At the risk of sounding conceited, I'm going to tell you anyway because it's important.

Objectively speaking, traveling the world does make you a better person. Let's not get hung up on whether it makes you a better person than the person standing next to you; the point is that it makes you a better person than you were before. Here are 5 reasons why:

1. Traveling humbles you and teaches you new things. As children we learn how to navigate the world by mimicking the

people we're raised around. We don't question whether there's a better way to do things. We just assume that the way the people around us think and behave is the way to think and behave. The longer we repeat these thoughts and behaviors the more ingrained they become.

No doubt you know some old person who has been thinking and behaving the same way for so long that there's no hope of them ever changing even though it's obvious to you that they're hopelessly out of date. That's because the more ingrained our old patterns of thought and behavior (which we mimicked from the people around us) become the more invested we become in our culture. Now, every culture does some things better than others and some things worse than others. No matter how great your culture is, it's still incomplete. There are invaluable life lessons to be learned from other cultures that you could never possibly imagine because they're so far outside your experiences. The more you travel the more you see this, the more it breaks down your prejudices and preconceived notions, the more it opens your eyes.

A word of warning though, you'll never fit back into your original culture's mold after you've broken out of it. You'll go back home, and everything and everyone will be different. Actually, they'll be exactly the same. You just don't fit in anymore, and you never will.

2. Traveling teaches you how to adapt. I've heard stories about Americans flying to Germany, stepping off the plane and upon hearing everyone speaking a different language they freak out and board the next plane back to America. On the other hand, you can drop a world traveler in the middle of any city on the planet and they'll settle in and navigate their environment like a

special ops soldier dropped in the wilderness. This skill isn't just useful for getting dropped in a foreign city though. There are new experiences around every corner even in the city you've spent your entire life. If you consistently run from new experiences it cripples your ability to thrive in any environment. If you consistently accept the challenge of life it trains you to thrive in any environment and live proactively with self-determination instead of letting the tides of life bash you into the rocks.

3. Traveling makes you a more animated person. Every culture has its own idiosyncrasies, cultural nuances, stories and forms of art. How bland would your tastes be if the only food you ever ate was McDonald's? How bland would your style be if you only wore togas? How bland would your vocabulary be if you never heard a foreign word? How bland would your mind be if you never heard any stories except the ones of your ancestors? I lament the fact that there are so many places I've never been, so many people I've never met and so many stories I've never heard because I know that my personality is blander because of it. Yet I know people who have never left the county I graduated high school in, and they're proud as hell about it, but in the end, they're really just celebrating how mundane their life and thus their personality is.

4. Traveling gives you more complete perspective of how the world works. I once met a German who explained to me that America's fanatic patriotism is a mirror image of the same blind nationalism that handed Germany over to the Nazis. I once met a South African who explained to me that black Africans view African Americans as white. I once met an Australian who explained how "Australia looks towards America" and "New Zealand looks towards Europe." Even though it's obvious, I

never knew that the Vietnamese call the "Vietnam War," the "American War" until I visited the American war crimes museum in Ho Chi Minh City. I never knew what abject poverty was until I visited Cairo. I didn't understand globalization until I saw an Arab in full sheik robes walking through a mall in Kuwait City carrying two giant bags of KFC chicken. I never knew how sexually repressed America is until I went to a topless beach in Italy. Every culture you visit is another piece of the puzzle. The more you see, the more you'll understand. The less you've seen, the fewer pieces you'll have to work with, and the less empowered your mind will be.

5. Traveling makes you a more complete person. That's what all of this adds up to. "Knowing is half the battle." "The more you know, the more you grow." I can tell you all of this, and you can comprehend it rationally, but until you actually step out of your comfort zone and into a new world, you'll never truly understand it. Of course, this presents a conundrum. Even if you could visit every country in the world you still wouldn't have enough time to spend in each country to fully digest what each of them has to offer. So what does that mean? Are we doomed to ignorance and incompleteness? I suppose technically that's true, but I like to focus on the positive: each new experience makes you a better person than you were before, and becoming a more complete person is its own reward regardless of what happens tomorrow. The only question is how far you're going to take yourself.

ODE TO THE PUKEKO (AND EVERYTHING ELSE I NEVER KNEW EXISTED)

You experience a very special and rewarding sense of joy when you travel and get to see famous things like the Eiffel Tower or the pyramids of Giza. When you stand in front of a historical icon you've only ever read about in books or seen in movies you're lucidly aware of the fact that you get to tick a very popular item off of your bucket list. And before you get back on the tour bus you're already savoring the fact that for the rest of your life you can say, "Been there. Done that." or "At least I saw Venice." or "We'll always have Paris."

As triumphant as you may feel standing in front of something famous, you're only going to spend a small portion of your vacation time actually staring at old buildings. The rest of the time you're going to be riding in vehicles, eating at cafes, visiting shops, looking for beaches and hunting choice souvenirs. Everywhere you'll go you'll see tours and businesses advertised as "off the beaten track." And inevitably you'll get swept into doing something exotic you had no intention of doing like skydiving, bungee jumping, eating gelato, eating snake, drinking grappa, drinking kava, riding an elephant or soaking in a mineral mud bath. In a lot of ways, these are the vacation memories you'll savor most. Thirty years from now you're not going to say your spouse, "Man, remember the time we stood there and looked at that big, old building? Wasn't that great?" No. You're going to be talking about, "Remember that time you were riding on that elephant and it started humping that other elephant?"

It's worth the money to travel and collect experiences and memories of you doing silly, exotic things. It's even more worth the money when you stumble across something so foreign to you that you never had any idea it or anything like it ever existed. That's an exhilarating and humbling experience worth traveling the world for.

I felt like this the first time I ate lychee; there's this fruit that millions of people eat every day. It tastes really good, and it's way easier to peel than an orange. How did I never know this existed? Are there millions of people out there who have never seen or heard of anything like an orange? How many other things are there out there that I never knew about?

Once you've visited a couple of world famous monuments or cities the world starts feeling smaller and you don't feel so lost or isolated. You start feeling like an informed world citizen. And then someone puts an alien piece of fruit on your plate and it reminds you that you don't know shit about shit.

I get the same feeling every time I see a pukeko, which is a big blue chicken looking bird that runs wild all over New Zealand. They hang around campsites, and you'll see them on the side of the motorways. I probably see three or four pukekos a month, but if I lived in the country I'd see a lot more.

Every time I see a Pukeko I still marvel at how I spent 30 years of my life not knowing there were crazy blue chicken birds running around public parks snatching children's lollies. Pukekos may be a pest to some people, but to me, they're a symbol of knowledge and humility....or something like that. The point is I think pukekos are totally sweet and everyone should know about them.

AN EXPAT TRIES TO DEFINE HIS IDENTITY

The other day at work I had to fill out a typical bureaucratic piece of paperwork that, among other things, asked my ethnicity. It gave three options: European, Pacific Islander and Other. After some consideration, I checked the box next to "European." Shortly thereafter my boss (a British expat) cracked a little joke about how I checked the wrong box. I cracked a joke back saying that there wasn't a box for "Yankee"...even though technically (being from Texas) I'm not a Yankee, but few people outside America understand or care about the difference, and I gave up bothering to clarify it to them a long time ago. Anyway, technically the Brit was right. I'm not from Europe, but technically he was also wrong, because if you trace my ancestry back far enough my family tree traces back to Europe. So technically, I am of European descent. In fact, if I had to check an ethnicity box on a bureaucratic form in America the "correct" answer would be: "white American of European descent."

This little episode got me reminiscing on my genealogy. My mother's side of my family comes from France, but my father's side is a little more complicated. They come from Haan, a village in Holland near the German border. So you could say that side of my family is Dutch, but the border of Holland and Germany has swayed over the centuries. So depending on which year you trace my family history back to I could either be Dutch or German. This raises the question, how far back do you have to trace your genealogy to find an accurate label for your heritage?

Let's take the question to its inevitable conclusion. Why not trace your genealogy all the way back? Many (if not most) historians hold that humanity originated in Africa. This means that, technically (despite my blonde hair and blue eyes), I'm an African American....but that's still assuming the country I was born in (America) is a critical benchmark for defining one's identity.

As cut and dry as that measurement seems, many people would still find fault with it. Since culture is based more on the way people live and think than political boundaries, many Texans identify themselves as "Texan" first and "American" second. Even then, what is an American? Everyone in South America is technically American. Canadians live in North America. So they're American too. And what's a Native American? The "Indians" who lived here before Europeans invaded came from Asia. So technically, they should be called Asian Americans, but again, if you go back far enough you could technically call them African Americans as well. For that matter, if you go back even farther down the evolutionary trail you could say we're all sea people. If you go even farther back we're all star dust.

But getting back to the present, the question of my personal cultural identity gets murkier still when you factor in that I spent 7 years in the US military, which has a culture all its own. Many veterans spend so long in the military that they identify primarily as a veteran and view regular US citizens as a group distinctly separate from theirs. I didn't buy into the system that much...well, maybe a little...but at any rate, I was in the service long enough to adopt a certain amount of military culture. On top of that, I was stationed in Italy, Germany and Hawaii for 2-3 years per assignment. Living abroad in those other cultures left an indelible mark on my psyche, and today I wouldn't be who I am without the experiences I had within those other cultures. If being raised in Texas makes me a Texan then living in Italy, Germany and Hawaii makes me culturally part Italian, German and Hawaiian. However, many of the native people who were born in each of those places viewed me as an unwelcome outsider and wanted me to leave. Should I let their prejudices influence how I'm allowed to define myself?

This is one of the things traveling the world does to you. It forces you to reexamine all the labels and assumptions of identity you were raised to take for granted, and the inevitable conclusion you're bound to come to in regards to ethnicity is that our place of birth is arbitrary. Who you are is defined by what you've experienced, not by the place on your birth certificate. At any rate, the culture that exists in that time and place you were born only exists as it does because countless people have migrated from around the globe to the place you were born after intertwining the knowledge they learned from every person their ancestors have ever come into contact with. They then used that knowledge to help them survive in an ever changing environment, and as their environment changed they changed along with it. So nobody's culture is the benchmark of reality. It's like scooping a glass of water out of a river and saying that this glass of water is what a river is supposed to be. And since the river is constantly flowing I couldn't just say "I'm a Texan" because what it means to be a Texan changes every year as the culture there evolves. So if I were to identify as a Texan I would have to add a conditional statement giving the years I spent in Texas. But if we have to get this surgical about it then we have to ask ourselves, why bother? Why is it so friggin important to find the right box to fit ourselves into and label ourselves with?

The more you travel the world and the longer you live abroad the more you're inclined to come to the conclusion (hopefully) that our differences are arbitrary. In the end, we're all humans who evolved from the same roots. We're all one global culture sharing the same physical and intellectual resources. There's not really any such thing as a Texan or an American or a Kiwi or an Italian or Russian or Fijian. There are only human beings stranded on an absurd, beautiful little dirt ball spiraling around an explosive ball of burning hydrogen gas that's hurtling through the emptiness of space. To put it simply, we're all in the same boat. We're all just human. That's the most accurate label I can come up with.

INDIANA JONES AND THE SORCERER'S STONE

I have this philosophy I call, "The Indian Jones and the Sorcerer's Stone Principle." If you're from the United Kingdom you could call it the "Indiana Jones and the Philosopher's Stone Principle." The theory goes like this:

Have you ever watched a movie like Indiana Jones, Harry Potter or Star Wars and thought how awesome it would be to live a life filled with so much adventure? If Hollywood has done its job right then the answer to that question should be, "yes."

Take a step back and watch those exciting action movies closely though. From beginning to end almost nothing good happens to the hero. Most of the adventure is one turn for the worse after the other. If there's not a giant boulder about to crush you there's a three-headed dog trying to eat your arms. Action movies are really pretty morbid when you think about it. Then again, they're only painful to the hero during the moment. When it's all said and done and all the trials are past it's the hardships that make the journey epic. It's the unexpected turns for the worse that bring flavor to the journey, and when you look back on the journey it's the things that went wrong that you laugh about the hardest and longest.

Have you ever seen a movie where everything goes right? Unless it was pornographic it would be too boring to sit through. Even then...but I digress.

Every time I go on a vacation I can't wait to see what goes wrong next. I've started a couple of trips with no plan and no map just to make sure nothing goes as planned, and when events really do take a turn for the worst in a way that could be viewed as regrettable I try to remind myself that I'm going to be laughing about it later. So I may as well start now.

If you ever plan on doing extensive traveling you'd be wise to start your journey with some version of the "Indiana Jones and the Sorcerer's Stone Principle" in the forefront of your mind. Even if you never do any traveling and spend your whole life in your hometown you'd still do well to keep this simple fact of life in mind: you can only have so much fun when everything goes right.

Made in the USA
Monee, IL
16 August 2020